A GLOSSARY
OF
PSYCHOANALYTIC TERMS AND CONCEPTS

Edited by
BURNESS E. MOORE, M.D.
BERNARD D. FINE, M.D.

Associate Editors
MARK KANZER, M.D.
BERNARD L. PACELLA, M.D.
GEORGE H. WIEDEMAN, M.D.

Second Edition

The Committee on Public Information
and
The Committee on Indexing

THE AMERICAN PSYCHOANALYTIC ASSOCIATION
One East 57th Street
New York, N. Y. 10022

Second edition, 1968

Second Printing, 1971

CONTENTS

CONTRIBUTORS

SAMUEL ABRAMS, M.D.
RENATO J. ALMANSI, M.D.
LEON L. ALTMAN, M.D.
STUART S. ASCH, M.D.
LEOPOLD BELLAK, M.D.
FRANK BERCHENKO, M.D.
DAVID BERES, M.D.
ISIDOR BERNSTEIN, M.D.
HAROLD P. BLUM, M.D.
CHARLES BRENNER, M.D.
BERNARD BRODSKY, M.D.
AARON COLEMAN, M.D.
JOSEPH T. COLTRERA, M.D.
ROBERT DICKES, M.D.
KURT R. EISSLER, M.D.
JEROME ENNIS, M.D.
AARON H. ESMAN, M.D.
LEON FERBER, M.D.
STEPHEN K. FIRESTEIN, M.D.
CHARLES FISHER, M.D.
MAX FORMAN, M.D.
HENRY M. FOX, M.D.
MAURICE R. FRIEND, M.D.
JOHN FROSCH, M.D.
MANUEL FURER, M.D.
GEORGE GERO, M.D.
SANFORD GIFFORD, M.D.
PAUL H. GRAY, M.D.
RALPH R. GREENSON, M.D.
IRVING B. HARRISON, M.D.
ERNEST HARTMANN, M.D.
PETER T. JANULIS, M.D.
EDWARD D. JOSEPH, M.D.
SYLVAN KEISER, M.D.
JUDITH S. KESTENBERG, M.D.
HEINZ KOHUT, M.D.
DAVID LEACH, M.D.
JEROME M. LEVINE, M.D.
HEINZ LICHTENSTEIN, M.D.
ROY K. LILLESKOV, M.D.
THEODORE LIPIN, M.D.
HANS W. LOEWALD, M.D.
RUDOLPH M. LOEWENSTEIN, M.D.
LEO S. LOOMIE, M.D.
ERNEST MARCUS, M.D.
IRWIN M. MARCUS, M.D.
JOHN B. McDEVITT, M.D.
ARNOLD H. MODELL, M.D.
DOUGLAS W. ORR, M.D.
MORTIMER OSTOW, M.D.
JOSHUA M. PERMAN, M.D.
LEO RANGELL, M.D.
GEORGE A. RICHARDSON, M.D.
SAMUEL RITVO, M.D.
LEWIS L. ROBBINS, M.D.
HERMAN ROIPHE, M.D.
NATHANIEL ROSS, M.D.
DAVID L. RUBINFINE, M.D.
OSCAR SACHS, M.D.
HOWARD H. SCHLOSSMAN, M.D.
HERBERT T. SCHMALE, M.D.
MAX SCHUR, M.D.
NATHAN P. SEGEL, M.D.
CALVIN F. SETTLAGE, M.D.
LEONARD L. SHENGOLD, M.D.
LEO A. SPIEGEL, M.D.
RICHARD F. STERBA, M.D.
WALTER A. STEWART, M.D.
HERBERT F. WALDHORN, M.D.
MARTIN WANGH, M.D.
JOSEPH WEISS, M.D.
EMANUEL WINDHOLZ, M.D.
RICHARD V. YAZMAJIAN, M.D.
ELIZABETH R. ZETZEL, M.D.

INTRODUCTION

The publication of Sigmund Freud's *Interpretation of Dreams* at the turn of the century marked the significant beginning of the still relatively new science of psychoanalysis. Since then, despite the skepticism with which psychoanalysis was received initially, the systematized body of knowledge built on Freud's structure has become the most important theoretical framework for an explanation of the psychology of human behavior. Freud's writings are still a vital and enlightening source of information about the dynamics of emotions and mental processes, read by students of psychoanalysis and laymen alike. Nevertheless, although psychoanalytic terms have for a long while been assimilated into the everyday language of modern intellectual life, their usage often conveys a superficial and sometimes distorted understanding of their meaning. It could scarcely be otherwise. What is read most widely are Freud's earlier works, which contain some of his most significant and startling discoveries, but it is not commonly realized that they reflect a science in *statu nascendi.* His theory underwent considerable revision through the years, and terms and concepts which were originally undifferentiated became gradually more specific, while their original ambiguous usage persisted. Freud was a master of German prose, as the Goethe Prize for Literature awarded to him in 1930 attests, but English translations of his works were poor until Strachey undertook the editing of the definitive *Standard Edition.* Even now, some of the precision of his terminology is inevitably lost in translation. Psychoanalysis has always attracted casual readers who have little opportunity or time to search out the meaning intended. In recent years a flood of psychoanalytic books, originally intended for professional communication, has been made available to the general public; terms in common usage, which have, however, been given specific technical meanings, add to misunderstanding and confusion. Contributing to this problem has been the lack of an easily accessible, reasonably brief, yet authoritative reference.

This small book represents an attempt by organized psychoanalysis to clarify for the public in simple, understandable language what is meant by its terms and concepts. It is a public information effort initiated by the Committees on Public Information and Indexing, and enthusiastically supported by the American Psychoanalytic Association and its members. Over seventy contributors have submitted definitions on the basis of their special knowledge. The editors wish to acknowledge these basic contributions and express appreciation for the cooperation they received. Such devoted collaboration is a rewarding experience in a highly individualistic group. A few special acknowledgements are deserved and gratefully given: to the Executive Committee and Council for their support and encouragement; to Dr. Martin Stein, past Chairman of the Board on Professional Standards, from whose description of the functions of the Board we have borrowed; to Drs. Joseph Coltrera and Max Forman, and to Mr. Glenn Miller and Miss Liselotte Bendix, Librarians of the Chicago and New York Psychoanalytic Institutes respectively, for bibliographic assistance; and to Mrs. Helen Fischer, Executive Secretary of the Association, and her staff, who met the many demands of this project with efficiency and good humor.

The glossary is intended to be a brief compendium of major psychoanalytic concepts and frequently encountered terms. The usual format has been employed. Words printed in italics are defined elsewhere in the glossary. Words in the text in bold face are terms subsumed under the heading of the major concept being defined, or ones which have been briefly but sufficiently defined in the context. An index is provided for those terms not separately defined.

B. E. M.

B. D. F.

THE AMERICAN PSYCHOANALYTIC ASSOCIATION

The American Psychoanalytic Association is the national organization of medical psychoanalysts in the United States. Now the largest regional body of psychoanalysts in the world, the Association includes over 1200 members, twenty-nine affiliate societies, and twenty-one training institutes. Although fully autonomous, it is the only psychoanalytic organization in this country affiliated with the International Psycho-Analytical Association, which automatically accepts members of the American Psychoanalytic Association.

As one of the component organizations of the American Association for the Advancement of Science, the American Psychoanalytic Association maintains contact with general science, while its membership in the World Federation for Mental Health evidences a continuing interest in the international trends in this important field. The close relationship between psychoanalysis and psychiatry in this country is reflected in the associated conventions and joint meetings of the American Psychoanalytic and American Psychiatric Associations, which began in 1934.

The purpose of the Association is to study and advance psychoanalysis; to advocate and maintain standards for the training of psychoanalysts and the practice of psychoanalysis; to foster the integration of psychoanalysis with other branches of medicine and to encourage research in all fields having to do with the scientific knowledge and welfare of man. Semi-annual meetings in May and December are devoted to these scientific and organizational aims. The meetings provide a forum for the presentation of clinical studies and the advancement of new theoretical ideas, and for the continuing post-graduate education of members through discussions at scientific panels and in small seminar groups.

In its provision of a Board on Professional Standards, charged with responsibility for initiating and fostering new training facilities, setting and maintaining standards of training for approved institutes, and certifying the qualifications of applicants for membership, the Association is almost unique among professional organizations. Membership in the Association, because of the high standards required, has come to be recognized as a form of accreditation for psychoanalysts —in fact, the only form existent.

The educational and training responsibilities of the Board are discharged by Committees on New Training Facilities, on Institutes, Membership, Child Analysis, Research Training, and Psychoanalytic Education. The latter committee, unburdened by administrative responsibility, has acted as a clearing house and originator of studies in the field of psychoanalytic education. Its functions complement those of other committees, and its study interests have included basic principles, curriculum, supervision, selection of candidates, the training analysis, and psychoanalytic pedagogy.

Since many local, historical, and socio-cultural factors affect the training given in the various institutes, the Board on Professional Standards can only establish minimally acceptable standards for the basic elements of psychoanalytic education. However, as the affiliate institutes have themselves established acceptable standards over the years, the Board has become more a forum for the discussion of issues in psychoanalytic education, for the questioning of old practices and the establishment of new, improved methods for the education of candidates. Its committees have become study and research groups in psychoanalytic education, and its administrative functions have played an increasingly secondary role.

The interest of the Association in training and education is carried over into the post-graduate field. An active Committee on Post-Graduate Development has studied the scientific programs of the various societies, the formation of small study groups, and the research activities of members, and is actively promoting these activities, which foster the continuing scientific interest and development of the individual analyst. A Committee on Indexing has been working over the past several years to clarify terminology and facilitate the ready availability of psychoanalytic knowledge. A Liaison Committee with South and Central American psychoanalytic organizations played a major role in the organization of the First Pan-American Congress for Psychoanalysis in Mexico City in 1964 and the Second in Buenos Aires in 1966.

Looking beyond its own organizational, professional, and scientific interests, the Association maintains a Committee on Public Information to cooperate with the news media and assist in the interpretation of its scientific activities. A pilot survey of the analytic and extra-analytic professional activities of its members has been conducted to define their contribution to mental health programs and community psychiatry, and this survey is being extended to cover the entire membership. A Committee on Social Problems is attempting to compile the psychoanalytic knowledge applicable to the prevention of mental disease and is studying the relevancy of psychoanalysis to current social problems, such as juvenile delinquency, alcoholism, drug addiction, and sexual deviations, and the relationship of psychoanalysts to community psychiatry. Seventeen centers connected with institutes offer low-cost analytic treatment. A number of Extension Schools present courses for other medical groups, social workers, educators, and law enforcement officers, bringing to them psychoanalytic knowledge that may be useful in their work with the emotional problems that beset mankind.

Minimal Standards For Training

Psychoanalytic training is a function of approved training institutions of the American Psychoanalytic Association, and not of any analyst as an individual. The Board on Professional Standards has established minimal standards which constitute a uniform policy for the training facilities of the American Psychoanalytic Association. These standards, briefly presented below, relate to 1) the requirements for eligibility of applicants; 2) the basic aspects of psychoanalytic training; and 3) eligibility for membership in the American Psychoanalytic Association.

1) Applicants for training must have graduated from a class A medical school and have completed one year's medical interneship and at least one year's residency training in psychiatry at institutions approved by the Council on Medical Education and Hospitals of the American Medical Association or at foreign institutions of equivalent rating. Under special circumstances, students from non-medical disciplines may be accepted for research training.

2) The basic elements of the training program include a personal analysis, a required curriculum of study, and the conduct of analyses under supervision.

A preparatory personal analysis is required for the purpose of freeing the candidate from emotionally conditioned attitudes which may interfere with psychoanalytic therapeutic work. In addition to its therapeutic benefit, the preparatory analysis provides the student with first-hand experience with unconscious mental phenomena and the process of analysis. Experience has shown that at least 300 hours of analysis, often much more, are required to fulfill this purpose.

The basic curriculum, usually begun in the year after the start of the preparatory analysis, includes study of psychoanalytic literature, lectures, seminars, and supervised clinical experience to impart an understanding of the fundamentals of psychoanalysis as developed by Freud and his co-workers. Continuing developments in the field are studied on the basis of this foundation. Organized reading and seminars, continuous case seminars, and clinical conferences are offered throughout at least three, usually four or more, years of training.

During his training, the student is required to analyze under supervision no less than two adult cases, at least one of which is to be carried through the terminal phase of analysis. A minimum of at least 150 hours of such supervision by two supervisory analysts other than his own training analyst is considered barely adequate to attain the aims of supervision. These are instruction in the use of the psychoanalytic method, the acquisition of therapeutic skill, and adequate observation of the candidate's work to determine how fully his personal analysis has achieved its aims.

Specialization in child analysis requires advanced instruction in the analysis of children in addition to completion of the training requirements for adult analysis.

3) Certification regarding the satisfactory completion of a candidate's training by his training institute makes the graduate eligible to apply for membership in the American Psychoanalytic Association. Acceptance automatically confers the same privileges in the International Psycho-Analytical Association.

A Brief Historical Note

Ernest Jones, later Freud's biographer, and A. A. Brill, the first American translator of Freud's work, organized the first meeting of the American Psychoanalytic Association in May, 1911, only a year after the International Psycho-Analytical Association was founded. Since then the Association has undergone three phases of development. From 1911 to 1932 it was a loose organization of individual members without any specific requirements for training in psychoanalysis. Informal training was begun in New York in 1922, but it was not until 1931 that the New York Institute became the first such training organization in this country. Within the next two years local societies had been formed and institutes founded in Chicago, Boston, and the Washington-Baltimore area as well.

In 1932 the first Association was dissolved, and a federation of constituent societies with extensive local autonomy was established, which by 1938 included seven societies. As a result of Nazi persecution, a tremendous emigration of teaching analysts from Europe to America greatly strengthened training in this country, while that in Europe suffered correspondingly. The American Psychoanalytic Association, therefore, became independent of the International Training Commission and formulated for the first time its own minimal standards for the training of psychoanalysts. A bulletin was started, and an official roster became available.

A resolution against the future training of laymen for the therapeutic practice of psychoanalysis was passed in 1938, and incorporated in the by-laws when the Association was reorganized again in 1946. The wisdom of this decision has been hotly debated, and the restriction has been a source of considerable conflict, since the contributions of many non-medical psychoanalysts have been generally acknowledged to be outstanding. The 1946 reorganization also made the Association one of individual members, voting on a national basis, with affiliate rather than constituent societies. Institutes no longer were tied to societies, and five have been established in connection with universities. The increase in the number of analysts made it possible to have more than one institute and society in large cities. New York now has three approved institutes, Philadelphia and Los Angeles two each.

The total membership of the Association at key intervals illustrates its rapid growth. There were 92 members in 1932, 273 in 1945, 485 in 1953, 1,221 in 1967 and 1255 in 1968. Nevertheless, because of the special qualifications and long training necessary, the number of psychoanalysts will remain relatively limited. Through many years, they have constituted about nine per cent of the members of the American Psychiatric Association. Specific criteria determine the use of psychoanalysis as a therapy. In those mental conditions for which it is indicated, primarily the psychoneuroses and character neuroses, its therapeutic usefulness has been repeatedly demonstrated, but the classical procedure is not suited to all forms of mental disorder. As an investigative technique, however, it has provided knowledge helpful in understanding the mental processes encountered in psychoses and other serious psychopathological conditions as well as the mental mechanisms adaptively used in the course of normal human development. Applied to the data of other sciences, the arts, and the humanities, psychoanalysis has been productive in providing new insights and deeper understanding.

INDEX OF GLOSSARY TERMS

INDEX OF GLOSSARY TERMS

INDEX OF GLOSSARY TERMS

ACTING-OUT: The tendency of some persons to reproduce forgotten memories, attitudes, and conflicts by actions rather than words without conscious awareness or recognition of the fact. In the course of psychoanalytic treatment a patient may, for instance, act in a defiant way towards the therapist without being aware that this behavior reproduces past attitudes towards parental authority. This type of behavior is called 'acting out in the *transference*.' Quite often feelings towards the analyst are projected on to persons in the patient's everyday life, and acting out occurs outside the *analytic situation* but is related to it. Usually a manifestation of unconscious *resistance* to treatment, acting out is occasionally useful in facilitating the recovery of a forgotten traumatic incident or period of life. Some persons tend to externalize their conflicts through acting out without relevance to treatment. Sexual and aggressive wishes or defenses against such wishes are expressed in acting-out behavior, which often occurs in the course of adolescence and in various *character disorders*. Although certain sexual and aggressive acts in everyday life, self-damaging or harmful to others, have an unclear relationship to acting-out, the term is often applied in a pejorative and indiscriminate way to any aggressive or anti-social activity. It therefore lacks precision except in the context of the analytic situation.

ACTIVE-PASSIVE: An important polarity governing mental life which has various applications. Most commonly the terms apply to opposing aims of the instinctual drives. Activity is manifested when a person seeks an object upon which to gratify sexual or aggressive needs. Passivity is inherent in the wish to have another gratify instinctual needs on the *self*, to be the object of loving or aggressive attention, even though effort may have to be exerted to seduce or provoke such activity. In the course of normal development, the child increasingly performs functions actively which earlier were performed for him by adults, and a gradual change from passivity to activity is evident in locomotion, feeding, the development of language, and the control of impulses. By actively repeating in dreams, memory, fantasy, thought, affect, and action what has been experienced passively before, whether pleasant or unpleasant, the ego attempts to achieve mastery over internal and external stimuli—to be able to produce and control cause and effect. A specialized but significant psychoanalytic usage is in respect to the *structural concepts*—*id, ego,* and *superego*—which are conceived of as active or passive at various times and in relation to each other. For example, the ego takes an active role in relation to the id when it maintains control over the discharge of instinctual drives that are part of the id. If overwhelmed by an instinctual upsurge, the ego passively experiences the discharge. Although activity is often equated with masculinity and passivity with femininity, in respect to sexual expression this usage is considered imprecise and misleading.

'ACTUAL NEUROSIS': Since the German 'aktual' means 'present day', Freud used this term to categorize certain symptoms he believed to be physiological reactions to current faulty sexual practices and therefore not subject to analysis. He distinguished such symptoms from those of the *psychoneuroses (hysteria, phobias,* and *obsessional neurosis),* which are psychologically determined. Although a sexual basis was also postulated for the psychoneuroses, the contributory events and influences belong to the time of early childhood, and ideas and fantasies connected with these experiences have been forgotten (repressed) because of conflicts over forbidden wishes. When these conflicts are reactivated by a stimulus in adult life, *regression* occurs with *symptom formation* to protect against *anxiety.*

The two conditions designated as 'actual neuroses', **neurasthenia proper** and **anxiety neurosis,** were differentiated from Beard's concept of neurasthenia by Freud in 1894. With neurasthenia proper, which he attributed to excessive *masturbation,* Freud associated the symptoms of fatigue, headache, intestinal disturbances including constipation, tingling sensations (paresthesias), and sexual weakness. The clinical picture he described for anxiety neurosis included irritability, restlessness, states of anxious expectation, anxiety attacks, phobias, dizziness, tremor, sweating, breathing disturbances, rapid or irregular heart action, diarrhea, and sleep disorders. In patients with anxiety neurosis, sexual practices interfering with the frequency, rhythm, or quality of discharge appropriate to the individual—usually abstinence, genital excitation without relief, or coitus interruptus—were thought to disturb the equilibrium between psychical and somatic functions in the sexual act. Deflection of somatic sexual excitation from the psychical sphere presumably resulted in a damming up of *libido* and its expression as anxiety with accompanying visceral, motor, and autonomic manifestations. Thus, the concept of the 'actual neurosis' was associated with Freud's first or toxicologic theory of anxiety, which provided a physiological as opposed to a primarily psychological basis for symptoms.

'Actual neuroses' frequently occurred in combination with psychoneuroses; the symptoms were similar; and a distinction could be made only by psychoanalytic study. Although Freud reaffirmed his belief in the validity of the concept in his last work, other investigators have questioned the existence of 'actual neurosis' as a separate clinical entity. Freud's original observations on the relationship between anxiety and sexual arousal appear to be substantiated by clinical evidence, even though his first concept of anxiety as transformed libido was superseded by his later theoretical formulations. See *anxiety, neurosis, psychoneurosis.*

ADAPTATION involves the capacity to cope reasonably, yet advantageously, with the environment. While it requires conformity to the *reality* of the external world, it does not preclude activity directed toward its change. The term may refer to either the state of adaptedness which obtains between the organism and his environment, or the process of adaptation which brings about that state. Successful adaptation is regarded as one criterion of healthy ego functioning, which seeks to bring about a harmonious relationship between the *id, superego,* and external world. The ego fulfills the task of adaptation by intrapsychic changes or by modifications in the environment through activity. This accommodation should provide a gratifying, satisfactory discharge of instinctual forces within the limitations imposed by the external world and without pathological alterations of the ego itself. Adaptation has active and passive components and should not be confused with 'adjustment', an essentially passive phenomenon.

AFFECTS: Subjectively experienced feeling states, usually perceived as pleasurable or unpleasurable in relation to the gratification or frustration of instinctual drives, to realistic achievements, and to the fulfillment of ideals. There are physiologic components, usually expressed through somatic manifestations related to the functions under the control of the vegetative nervous system. Common examples are blushing, sweating, crying, increased peristalsis, rapid pulse, etc. The voluntary skeleto-muscular system, however, may be activated as well; posture, facial expression, and tone of voice being examples of bodily changes mediated by the peripheral nerves. A psychic component is regularly present and may exist with little or no physiological manifestation, as in the case of feelings of happiness or sadness.

Since affects are subjective experiences, they must be within conscious awareness and do not occur unconsciously in the same sense that other psychic phenomena do. Although the term 'unconscious affect' (e.g. guilt) is used, it is an abbreviated reference to a psychic state in which repressed (*unconscious*) ideas connected with forbidden wishes threaten to erupt into *consciousness,* thereby leading to the affect of guilt. This danger may be warded off in some instances by substituting a consequence, appropriate to the affect, for the affect itself. Thus some people put themselves into situations of being injured or punished without being aware that the behavior serves as an expiation for guilt.

AFFECTIVE DISORDERS: A diagnostic category of psychopathology in which exaggerated affective reactions are the main presenting symptoms. Not all affects are expressed in such extreme fashion; but depression, elation, or an alternation of depression and elation characterize the clinical states included in this term. The specific diagnostic entities are: psychotic depressive reaction, manic state, manic-depressive psychosis, involutional melancholia, and post-partum depression. From the psychoanalytic point of view, the essential feature of depression is the turning of the punitive tendencies of the *superego* against the *self,* whereas in mania the superego functions are largely suspended. In both instances *ego functions,* especially the sense of *reality,* are markedly impaired.

AGGRESSION: Means attack or hostile action. It may take the form of physical assault as one extreme, or gentle, implicit verbal criticism as the other. It also includes degradation by act or word, avoidance, teasing and provocation. In ordinary social life aggressive tendencies are, as a rule, restrained except for a few fairly well ritualized situations such as competitive sports, in which their expression is encouraged. In adults physical aggression that is not a response to a clear threat or unusual provocation occurs mainly in persons with mental illness or character disorders. In such instances, the escape of aggression is to be attributed either to a pathologic intensification of the aggressive tendencies, a pathologic weakness of the controls, or both. In some forms of mental illness, aggression may be turned against the *self* and lead to self-damaging acts or suicide. Often aggressive behavior is combined with its natural opponent, affectionate behavior, so as to yield sadistic or masochistic acts. Psychoanalysts assume that there is an aggressive *instinctual drive* (q.v.) underlying all manifestations of aggression, and that it is instrumental, together with the *libidinal drive,* in the formation of psychic structures. See *Instinctual Drives.*

AMBIVALENCE: Describes the simultaneous existence of opposite feelings, attitudes, and tendencies directed toward another person, thing, or situation. In this most general sense, ambivalence is universal and not significant because there are very few affectionate relations which are uncomplicated by some hostility, and many hostile relations are tempered by affection. When, however, the strength of these conflicting feelings increases to the point where action seems unavoidable yet inacceptable, some defensive maneuver is undertaken which often leads directly to mental illness. Under these circumstances, the ambivalence is repressed, that is, only one of the two sets of feelings is permitted to become conscious. Usually it is the hostility which is repressed, but sometimes it is the affection. Successful psychoanalytic detection of the repressed component of the ambivalence, and its successful demonstration to the patient, will usually exert a therapeutic influence.

AMNESIA: An inability consciously to recall past experiences, and the psychic and emotional reactions accompanying them. Although amnesias can result from ordinary processes of forgetting, organic factors such as brain injury, or the toxic effects of drugs, the term in psychoanalytic usage usually refers to the effect of a repression which actively removes from memory experiences which were traumatic in nature and very disturbing to the individual. Such unconscious defensive repression can occur at any age and interrupt the continuity of mental life, but the most significant amnesia relates to early childhood when the immaturity of the ego contributes to the traumatic effect of events **(i.e. infantile amnesia).** One of the major goals of psychoanalytic treatment is to lift amnesias, especially those of early childhood, and to permit the patient consciously to re-experience and master events which were overwhelming at the time. See *Trauma.*

ANACLITIC DEPRESSION: A syndrome appearing in infants in the second half of the first year of life. It was first described by Spitz and Wolfe in 1946. It manifests itself in weepiness, apprehension, withdrawal, refusal to eat, sleep disturbances, and eventually stupor. The causal factor is the removal of the mothering person without provision of a suitable substitute for the infant. Spitz considers the condition an infantile version of the adult depressive *psychosis.* If the mother (or a mothering person) is made available within three months, the child usually recovers quickly from the *depression.* The term 'anaclitic' refers to the 'leaning-on' quality of the infant's relationship to the mother, as the person who nourishes and cares for him, and is the central object of the infant's *instinctual drives.*

ANALITY: A broad term referring to the psychic organization of all the sensations, impulses, and personality traits derived from the **anal stage** of *psychosexual development.* This period, roughly between one and three years of age, is marked by recognizable emergence of the aggressive drive, admixed with the libidinal in sadistic impulses; the acquisition of voluntary sphincter control; an increasing shift from passivity to activity; and a concomitant *ambivalence* toward the mother with a struggle for separation, individuation, and independence. **Anal erotism** refers to sexual pleasure in anal functions, which may have a quality derived from touching, smelling, withholding, or expelling. In later life it may appear in disguised or sublimated forms.

Adaptive and maladaptive character traits, often seemingly inconsistent, are derived from anal erotism and defenses against it. Orderliness, obstinacy, frugality, and parsimony are features of the **anal character,** for whom anal function has had an exaggerated significance. Heightened ambivalence, untidiness, defiance, rage, and sadomasochistic tendencies stem from the anal phase when defenses are less adequate. Various aspects of the *obsessive-compulsive neurosis* also represent anal fixations.

ANALYTIC PROCESS: In an inclusive sense this term refers to psychoanalysis as a psychotherapeutic method which includes three phases: 1) the establishment of the *analytic situation* (q.v.); 2) the emergence and interpretation of the *transference neurosis* (q.v.); 3) the *working through* of the terminal phase. Certain aspects of all three phases are not specific to psychoanalysis; they may be recognized in all types of individual psychotherapy. However, it is only in classical psychoanalysis that the setting and the method deliberately encourage the type and degree of *regression* which results in the affectively charged re-emergence of unresolved childhood conflicts in the current relationship between patient and analyst.

The essence of the analytic process is to be regarded as the patient's achievement of greater insight, mastery, and progressive maturity through the subjective experience in the *transference neurosis* and its interpretation in the *analytic situation.*

ANALYTIC SITUATION: The setting in which the process of psychoanalysis takes place. It is a one to one relationship between analyst and patient, and differs from other forms of psychotherapy in that it imposes certain specific demands and frustrations. The patient is required to recline in a position where the analyst cannot be seen, and to report freely and without exception all his thoughts and feelings, suspending any critical and logical selection that is taken for granted in the usual social situation. Deprivation, both sensory and affective, is often experienced by the patient if, when it is appropriate, the analyst remains silent and seemingly unresponsive. These conditions encourage regression in the patient with re-emergence of repressed infantile wishes, fantasies, and memories. A positive basic relationship between analyst and patient, i.e. a **therapeutic alliance,** has to be maintained to safeguard the analytic situation if a successful resolution of the *transference neurosis* is to be achieved.

ANXIETY: A distressing *affect* (feeling tone) which is subjectively experienced as worry similar to fear of a real danger or its anticipation. Anxiety, however, is said to be 'free-floating' if it exists without conscious reference to a specific external danger. It is usually accompanied by objective manifestations of increased activity of those bodily functions under the control of the autonomic (vegetative) nervous system, resulting, for instance, in palpitations, fast breathing, sweating, diarrhea, etc.

Anxiety is of crucial theoretical importance in psychoanalysis. Its significance lies in the fact that the mental conflicts which cause neurotic symptoms are believed to be due to unconscious fantasies of punishment for instinctual wishes originating in childhood. There are typical dangers *(conscious* in early childhood, *unconscious* later on) that gave rise to fear and to neurotic *conflict*. These are: 1) loss of or separation from a person on whom the child depends for care and love (object loss); 2) anger or disapproval on the part of such a person (loss of love); 3) loss of or damage to the genitals (castration complex); and 4) bad conscience (guilt, *superego* anxiety, based on disapproval of oneself on the basis of one's own internalized moral standards).

As a part of normal *ego functioning,* anxiety may serve the purpose of alerting the individual to a danger, the result of unconscious conflict. The ego then initiates unconscious defensive operations to ward off consciousness of the unacceptable instinctual wishes. If this **signal anxiety** fails in its purpose. symptoms may result, persistent or recurrent anxiety being one.

ANXIETY HYSTERIA: A psychopathological syndrome involving phobic and obsessive symptoms accompanied by a specific type of rigid character structure. The phobic symptoms are attacks of *anxiety* precipitated by exposure to, or even anticipation of, various external situations, in reality not dangerous or insufficiently so to warrant the degree of fear exhibited. In patients with this type of *psychoneurosis* it is usually possible to elicit the history of an acute anxiety attack immediately prior to the formation of the phobia. This anxiety is a precipitate and repetition of a traumatic experience in early childhood, often related to conflicts of the incestuous *phallic phase* although preoedipal fears are also of significance. The conditions under which the fear situation is generated may unconsciously represent punishment, such as loss of love (being shunned or abandoned), castration (injury to the body), or guilt (disapproval by the *superego*), for forbidden instinctual impulses. Hysterical and obsessional mechanisms may be utilized to cope with the anxiety, or more stable defenses may contribute to the character structure, such as counter-phobic attitudes. In the latter instance, the psychic experience of fear has itself been repressed, complicating diagnosis. The most characteristic feature, however, is the *phobia,* a special way of dealing with anxiety by creating new and less frightening dangers by **displacement** and **projection.** By limiting the anxiety to a specific situation the patient is able to externalize the danger, denying its inner source. By avoiding the phobic situation, he prevents continuous unpleasant awareness of the feeling of anxiety which indicates the danger of eruption of unacceptable instinctual derivatives. Also called 'phobic neurosis'. See *phobia*.

'AS IF' PERSONALITY: A type of severe *character disorder* typified by the quality of appearing as if emotionally involved—as in love—although actually lacking that capacity. The 'as if' personality may appear normal to the casual observer, displaying emotions of love, sympathy and understanding, but his relationships and affective responses remain superficial. The disorder is based on a lack of stability in the earliest object relationships, so that insufficient differentation of the *self* from the *object* has occurred. Relationships are inconstant and based on an incomplete *identification* rather than object love; they remain at the level of satisfying the person's own needs rather than those of the object. The defective identificatory process interferes with the development of a sense of *identity,* which is bolstered by a mimicry of those people to whom the 'as if' person becomes attached. Aggressive tendencies may be masked by passivity and apparently friendly compliance, but opportunism is not deterred by *object loss.* There is enormous suggestibility, and kaleidoscopic changes in behavior reflect a labile shifting from one object, social group, or cause to another.

ATTENTION: The process of bringing some mental product (a percept of the external world, memory, idea, fantasy, feeling, etc.) to a level of awareness by the observing function of the *ego.* To accomplish this, the mental product is assumed to be temporarily imbued with an additional charge of *psychic energy,* the so-called *'attention cathexis.'* The attachment of this attention raises the mental product over a hypothetical threshold to awareness.

In theory, all mental products can have attention cathexis attached to them. In practice, the ease with which the mental product acquires *attention cathexis* varies, giving rise to distinctions between *conscious, pre-conscious,* and *unconscious.* Often effort has to be directed toward preconscious data for them to achieve attention, which may be fleeting. For instance, one is usually not conscious at a given moment of one's birthdate; yet if asked, one can call it to awareness or attention for a brief time.

ATTENTION CATHEXIS: The psychic (mental) energy attached to a mental formation that is necessary to raise it to the level of awareness. It is a theoretical construct, like the concept of *psychic energy,* to account for the clinical phenomenon of *attention.* The nature of this energy is unknown, but its existence is assumed since presumably some force is necessary to raise the mental product above a hypothetical threshold into *consciousness.*

BEATING FANTASY: A special form of *fantasy* arising in childhood, but often encountered in adult patients. Classically, it has a tripartite form: the earliest version consists of conscious imagining that a sibling is being beaten by father; a second version, that the person himself (or herself) is being beaten by father, remains *unconscious;* while the final version, a *conscious* one, conceives of someone being beaten by an authority figure. The last fantasy often accompanies childhood masturbatory activities. There is evidence to suggest that some form of this fantasy occurs in the course of everyone's development, but only in certain circumstances does it have a profound effect on later development. Various defenses may be established against the imagined implications of the fantasies, which may result in symptoms, character changes of a masochistic nature, or in actual sadomasochistic sexual practices.

BISEXUALITY: A term that describes the presence of somatic and psychological attributes of the male and female in the same individual. Biologically, the determination of sex is based on the presence of the proper combination of sex chromosomes in the cell from which the embryo develops, namely two x-chromosomes for the female and one x and one y chromosome for the male. Primary sexual differentiation depends on the ratio of male and female hormones in embryos. Any disturbance of this ratio, for instance, as the result of an abnormal number of chromosomes, may modify the morphology of the sexual organs and cause hermaphroditism.

Psychologically the source of bisexuality in the human is the tendency of all children to identify with various attributes of both parents, especially those that characterize gender *identity.*

The term is also applied to individuals whose confusion in sexual (or gender) identity results in alternating or simultaneous sexual activity with homosexual and heterosexual *objects.*

It should be emphasized (because of frequent misunderstanding) that bisexuality is a normal [universal] human characteristic, both biologically and psychologically. In psychological development, this is indicated in the various phases of *psychosexual development,* culminating in the positive and negative aspects of the *oedipus complex.* The resulting predominance of masculine or feminine attributes is often associated with activity or passivity, but these two polarizing concepts should be clearly differentiated. See *active-passive, infantile sexuality, oedipus complex, psychosexual development.*

BODY EGO: The core of the *ego,* which consists of the psychic representation of the surface of the body. At the time the term originated, the *structural theory* had not yet been formulated, and ego was synonymous with what is now called 'the *self*', although it also had connotations of a system of the *psychic apparatus* governing certain functions. 'Body ego' retains this undifferentiated double meaning, since there is evidence to support the hypothesis that, developmentally, ego functioning is based on the model of body function, i.e., the mind introjects —takes in, as in nursing—what is need-satisfying and pleasurable, and seeks to evacuate what is noxious or unpleasant. The 'body ego' therefore also refers to this primitive type of ego functioning.

BODY IMAGE: The mental representation of one's body at any moment. The *ego* constructs it from the visual perception and tactile exploration of the surface of one's body and sensations from the inner organs, skeleto-muscular system, and the skin. Depending on the person's instinctual or defensive needs, the body image at any time may be realistic or unrealistic. For example, a woman's body image may include an 'illusory penis' under the influence of her masculine wishes. See *penis envy*.

BORDERLINE STATE: A descriptive term referring to a group of conditions which manifest both neurotic and psychotic phenomena without fitting unequivocally into either diagnostic category. In many borderline states, neurotic symptoms of a hysterical, phobic, or obsessive-compulsive nature are observed and represent defenses against more regressive and primitive states. Some of these conditions have been called 'pseudoneurotic schizophrenia'. In borderline states, superficial *adaptation* to the environment and the ability to maintain *object relations* may be relatively intact; hence many *ego functions* are fairly well preserved. Yet there is a weakness in the defenses against primitive instinctual impulses and interference with the overall evaluation of *reality*, logical thinking, adaptation to the environment, and other aspects of ego functioning. Under stress the psychotic aspects may come to the fore, since the flexibility and adaptability of these patients are reduced. Patients of this nature often fail to recognize their difficulties as symptoms, and have no significant wish for help except on an emergency basis.

CASTRATION ANXIETY: See *anxiety*. The very great importance of castration anxiety (fear of genital loss or injury) was an early and unexpected discovery in the history of psychoanalysis. It is an integral part of the *oedipus complex*, and is a major source of conflict in the course of childhood development. As part of the oedipus complex it plays a large role both in neurotic symptoms in later life and in the formation of character traits, whether normal or abnormal. In adults the fear has usually been displaced from the genitals to other parts of the body, so that exaggerated fear of injury to any part is based to some degree on castration anxiety or its feminine counterpart: fear of penetration.

CATHARSIS: Refers to a technical procedure to facilitate the expression of emotion which the patient has either repressed or suppressed. In the early days of psychoanalysis it was considered of primary importance as a therapeutic method, but now its role has become secondary as the importance of *insight* and *working through* (q.v.) has gained recognition.

CATHEXIS: A term derived from the Greek 'Catechein, to occupy' by the translators of Freud for the German word 'Besetzung'. The dynamic nature of human psychic activity in *adaptation* and in *conflict,* with forces working together or in opposition, calls for a theory of energies. The theory assumes a *psychic energy* (which is not the same as physical energy) derived from biological needs and manifested in wishes and impulses. On the basis of this theory, human behavior, thought, and emotion are the resultant of the interaction of the basic impulses and the counter-action of the controlling functions of the psyche. The basic impulses are represented in the theory as 'drives' (German: Trieb) and classified as libidinal and aggressive. The term 'cathexis' denotes the investment of the psychic energy of a drive in a mental representation. The latter may be an image, a *symbol,* a *fantasy,* an idea or a concept and these, in turn, may be conscious or unconscious. Thus when we say that 'A cathects B' we mean that subject A invests in his mental representation of B the energies of his libidinal or aggressive drives. What would be observed would be fantasies of love or hate directed by A toward B.

CHARACTER: That aspect of **personality** (the image of the person and his ways of reacting perceived by others) which reflects the individual's habitual modes of bringing into harmony his own inner needs and the demands of the external world. It is a constellation of relatively stable and constant ways of reconciling conflicts between the various parts of the *psychic apparatus* to achieve adjustment in relation to the environment. Character therefore has a permanent quality that affects the degree and manner of drive discharge, defenses, *affects,* specific *object relationships,* and adaptive functioning in general. Although both neurotic symptoms and character traits are compromises between instinctual impulses and forces of the ego that try to direct and organize an appropriate gratification, or to postpone or block the *impulses* in response to restraining or inhibiting forces, symptoms do not fit into the customary mode of behavior and are experienced as alien to the character, i.e., they are **ego-dystonic,** not accepted as part of the *self.*

The **integrating, synthesizing,** and **organizing functions** of the ego are significantly involved in determining character. Through these functions stimuli and impulses are sifted and organized. Some are permitted to find expression directly while others are tolerated only in altered form. Permanent character traits are either perpetuations of original impulses in modified form, *sublimations* of them, or **reaction formations** against them. Thus, some character attitudes or traits are defenses, others not, but none are completely independent of instinctual conflicts. Certain character attitudes, which appear to be instinctual, nevertheless serve a defensive function; and the defenses are instituted not only against *id* impulses, but against affects, especially *anxiety,* and even against the defenses themselves. Whether character traits are healthy or pathological is not dependent on the instinctual gratification permitted or on the defenses against such gratification, but on the ego's capacity to achieve a degree of flexibility, mobility, and even reversibility within a framework of constancy, which will lead to optimal mental functioning.

Some character traits are specifically correlated with the phases of libidinal development associated with the *erogenous zones.* See *orality, anality.* Ambition and shame are often associated with **urethral erotism.** Recklessness, resoluteness, and self-assuredness may be reactions to castration fear; and pride and courage, bashfulness and timidity are other traits developed around the conflicts of the castration complex in the *phallic phase.* The genital character is an ideal concept associated with the overcoming of *ambivalence,* an end to reaction formation, and an increase in the ability to sublimate. See *ego development, ego functions.*

CHARACTER DISORDERS: A heterogenous group of pathological character disturbances which exhibit in common an habitual inflexibility of behavior patterns without marked subjective discomfort. Instead of discrete areas of symptomatic involvement, the entire personality is usually affected, especially those *ego functions* determining frustration tolerance, drive regulation, affective responses, and *object relationships.*

In the development of character disorders *intra-psychic* conflict has been resolved by stable reaction patterns which permit partial gratification of instinctual wishes under limiting conditions or necessitate total renunciation with accompanying severe inhibition in work and play. These rigid *character formations* are required to maintain a constant defense against instinctual impulses, the *affects* connected with them, especially anxiety and guilt, or situations which would provide the opportunity for forbidden gratification. The need for love, security, enhancement of self-esteem, or the satisfaction of passive longings may also be involved. The typical reactions may be elicited only by certain situations, or the attitudes may be nonspecific and indiscriminately exhibited toward anyone at any time. Rationalization of motives and idealization of behavior may obscure the pathological nature of the attitudes, traits, and reaction patterns; and the total result may be adaptive and secure important realistic gains for the individual, so that to him his behavior appears justified, reasonable, appropriate, and consciously determined. Therefore, unlike symptoms which are *ego-alien* artifacts in normal functioning, character disorders are usually **ego-syntonic,** and there is initially little motivation for change. Sufficient satisfaction of instinctual needs is provided without guilt or anxiety, and his behavior is less troublesome for the patient than for those around him. However, the character disorders betray themselves by fatigue, inhibitions in certain areas or in general, the cramped and rigid nature of their adjustment, or the occasional breaking through of warded off impulses directly or in distorted form. Repeated exposure to the personal and social consequences of his actions may require the individual to seek treatment. In that case, analysis of the character distortions is necessary, but this gives rise to anxiety and strong *resistance* before the nature of the instinctual impulses may be recognized and the childhood situations which provided a genetic basis for intrapsychic conflict may be recalled or reconstructed. With such arousal of anxiety, a phase of neurotic symptomatology may precede successful resolution of the conflicts.

The classification of character disorders is confused and lacking in consistency. Certain terms which are generally used in a descriptive sense have also been applied to specific syndromes. Thus, the heading of this definition is used to mean disorders (pathological disturbances) of character, but **character disorder** usually conveys the connotation of **sociopathic traits** (anti-social, delinquent, criminal behavior), and is close to the **personality disorder** or **psychopathic personality** of the standard psychiatric nomenclature. Although disorders of character can occur without specifically recognized symptoms, some degree of character distortion invariably accompanies symptomatic neuroses and may be considered an extension of the neurotic process. The mechanisms operative in the formation of character traits are similar to those contributing to the formation of various symptoms. Where there is such demonstrable similarity, but without symptoms, the character disturbance is often referred to as a **character neurosis,** and various types are designated by analogy to the neuroses: e.g., hysterical, phobic, and compulsive. Classical symptomatic neuroses seem to be decreasing in frequency, and character neuroses make up an increasingly larger portion of psychoanalytic practice. **Schizoid characters** exhibit mechanisms analogous to those of *borderline* and psychotic patients. **Cyclic characters** are oral in nature, characterized by conflicts between the *ego* and *superego,* and the mechanisms of their mood swings are similar to those in manic-depressive patients. Two little used, but confusing terms are **anxiety character** and **neurotic character.** The first was Ernest Jones' term for those persons who are so dominated by a tendency to react to all stimuli with anxiety that they have to defend themselves against anxiety in all relationships. Alexander used 'neurotic character' to designate patients whose lives consist of a succession of successes and failures related more to the need to relieve unconscious tension than to reality. Their behavior in ordinary life situations resembles the *acting out* of neurotic conflicts in analysis and has been termed 'living out' by some authors. Acting out during psychoanalytic treatment is a frequent occurrence among patients with character disorders of all types.

CHARACTER FORMATION: The process by which the individual develops stable patterns of thinking, feeling, and acting through the interaction of his biologically transmitted predispositions with the environment. It is determined by the resolution of *intrapsychic conflict* in relation to the inhibiting forces affecting the expression of *instinctual drives,* especially as such resolutions are affected by traumatic situations. Character formation therefore proceeds concomitantly with *ego development.* The method and manner by which the *ego* admits, repels, or modifies instinctual claims depend on the way in which the person has been taught to regard them by his environment. The environment — the parents at first — enforces specific frustrations, blocks certain modes of reaction to these frustrations, and facilitates others, suggesting certain ways of dealing with the conflicts between instinctual demands and fears of further frustrations. Through the *ego-ideal* and the *superego,* which evolve from the resolution of oedipal conflict, the environment even creates desires by setting up specific goals, and influences the values attached by the individual to particular ways of adjusting inner need to *external reality.* How a person is affected by his parents—who serve as models for ego development, ego-ideal, and superego formation through the processes of *introjection* and *identification* — is dependent on the stage of development at which crucial situations involving *trauma* and conflict arise; which of the parents' attitudes the child adopts; whether he imitates their positive behavior or their prohibiting attitudes. Inborn potentialities, including a disproportion between the sexual and aggressive *drives,* may also determine the outcome. Fixation and regression and other complex genetic and dynamic factors are therefore involved in determing whether conflicts are solved by reality-adjusted, well-integrated behavior leading to apparent normality or, in contrast, whether a neurotic compromise results in overt symptomatology or a **character neurosis.** Some character attitudes arise as an adjustment to a *neurosis,* and a reciprocal relationship develops between such attitudes and the neurotic symptoms, such traits often being a secondary elaboration of the neurotic symptoms.

COMPULSION: The repetitious urge to perform an action or a pattern of actions (in which case it may be called a ritual) which do not appear fully or adequately rational to the subject, but which can be resisted only at the cost of evoking strong *anxiety*.

CONFLICT-FREE EGO SPHERE: That area of ego functioning which is not involved in *intrapsychic conflict*. Such *ego functions* as *consciousness,* motility, *perception,* memory, and thought have from their onset a relative independence or **'primary autonomy'** from the *instinctual drives*. These functions tend to mature in accordance with the individual's biological potential. Other ego functions which arise out of conflict may in the course of development become free of such involvement and thus develop what has been termed a **'secondary autonomy'.** This is sometimes accompanied by a **'change of function'** which implies that the initial functional activity is superseded by a modified, more adaptive one.

CONFLICT, INTRAPSYCHIC: Conflict between opposing forces within the mind in contrast to that between the individual and the outside world. Such conflicts begin in childhood and persist throughout life, are inevitable and universal, constituting, from a psychoanalytic point of view, one of the most important dynamic factors underlying human behavior. Their outcome determines the basis of neurotic symptoms and inhibitions on the one hand, and of a wide variety of character traits, both normal and abnormal, on the other.

Since conflicts originate in childhood in connection with sexual and aggressive wishes, one of the first results of the application of the psychoanalytic method to the treatment of mental illness was the recognition of the importance of *infantile* (childhood) *sexuality,* and in particular of that aspect of it which is subsumed under the heading of the *oedipus complex*.

CONSCIOUSNESS: A state of awareness of *perceptions* coming from the outside world and from within the body and mind. Perceptions from within include the observation of our own thought processes and affective states. Consciousness thus is a purely subjective phenomenon whose data can be communicated to others only by means of language and behavior. It has also been described as a superordinate sense organ subject to stimulation by the perceptual data reaching the central nervous system. It is assumed that consciousness utilizes neutralized *psychic energy* in the form of *attention cathexis* (see *attention*). Conscious states are subject to alteration in sleep, fatigue and illness. Various drugs, including LSD, marijuana and alcohol, also affect the state of consciousness.

COUNTER-PHOBIC MECHANISMS: Are means by which the individual attempts to overcome impeding or embarrassing fears and *phobias*. Relationship of the motivation for action to the underlying fear, and the experiences, feelings, and *fantasies* to which the fear is directly or symbolically related, are *unconscious*. Through these mechanisms, the feared circumstance becomes one that is actively sought. Henceforth, pleasure is seemingly found in those situations in which formerly *anxiety* predominated. The counter-phobic activity is a means by which the *ego* seeks to master anxiety by repeatedly coping with the danger situation. Transforming what has been passively endured into activity is the basic ego process underlying the counter-phobic mechanism.

COUNTERTRANSFERENCE: Refers to the attitudes and feelings, only partly conscious, of the analyst towards the patient. These may reflect the analyst's own unconscious conflicts, and if he is not constantly aware of this, may affect his understanding and therapeutic handling of the patient. In countertransference, the analyst has displaced on to the patient attitudes and feelings derived from earlier situations in his own life; the process is analogous to *transference,* the patient's similar reaction to the analyst, an important instrument in analytic therapy. One of the cardinal purposes of the analyst's own analysis during his training is to make him aware of his own conflicts and their derivatives, so that they do not distort his therapeutic work with patients. The analyst's continuing scrutiny of his own countertransference feelings frequently provides correct clues to the meaning of the patient's behavior, feelings, and thoughts, and may facilitate more prompt *perception* of the patient's *unconscious.*

CONTRAINDICATIONS FOR ANALYSIS: Those features of the clinical picture of a patient, and of his basic personality pattern and total life situation, which tend to militate against the likelihood of successful utilization of analysis at a specific time. Any condition which would prevent or seriously interfere with the practical application of analysis would be a contraindication—for example, physical incapacitation sufficient to prevent attendance at sessions, the presence of medical, surgical or other problems requiring urgent attention, etc. In addition, certain trends which are part of a prospective patient's neurosis or character may tend to block or disrupt analysis, if present in sufficient number or intensity. Examples here would be strong self-punitive tendencies, uncontrollable impulsiveness, pathological lying, extreme *anxiety* or any undiminishable *resistance* to being in treatment.

CONVERSION: A complex psychopathological process which attempts to conceptualize the rather poorly understood "leap from the mind to the body". Historically it has been intimately and almost exclusively linked with *symptom formation* in *hysteria.*

Originally it was understood by Freud as "the transformation of psychic excitement into the chronic physical symptoms which characterize hysteria". More specifically, it represents the regressive process by which *unconscious* mental representations (esp. thoughts and fantasies) bring about somatic changes or dysfunctions in order to express in a distorted way the derivatives of repressed forbidden impulses as modified by the individual's defenses. These somatic changes expressed in symbolic body language (q.v., *hysteria, symbolism, symptom formation*) represent a compromise and composite of the forbidden libidinal and aggressive impulses and the defensive forces which bring about the distortion. Conversion is therefore part of an unconscious process leading toward hysterical symptom formation in which there is a predominantly phallic-exhibitionistic orientation, rooted in conflicts derived from the **oedipal phase** and centered around the problem of *castration anxiety.* In addition, it has been generally accepted (although recently challenged) that conversion symptoms occur almost exclusively in organs and functions under the control of the voluntary nervous and muscular systems (as contrasted with the involuntary muscular and autonomic nervous systems).

Conversion symptoms are not simply somatic expressions of affects, but are specific representations of unconscious thoughts and *fantasies* which can be uncovered and retranslated through analysis from their "somatic language" into their original word language; this "translation" has shown that the meaning of each conversion symptom is unique for every individual.

The recent broadening of the concept of conversion by F. Deutsch and L. Rangell suggests that conversion, as an active ego process, can occur throughout the entire range of psychopathology at any stage of libidinal and *ego development*. Max Schur has recently made another important linkage of conversion to the concepts of somatization and desomatization.

CRITERIA FOR ANALYSIS: Those features, noted under *indications* and *contraindications for analysis,* the assessment of which, on balance, determine the advisability of analysis as the treatment choice for a particular patient at a particular time. Sometimes used as synonymous with *indications for analysis.*

DEFENSE MECHANISMS: Defense is a general term used to describe the struggles of the *ego* to protect itself against danger. The danger arises because of the threat of eruption into consciousness of a repressed wish which has become associated with some real or imagined punishment. This is signalled by painful feelings of *anxiety* or guilt, and these feelings impel the ego to ward off the wish or *drive.* Defense always operates unconsciously so that the person is unaware of what is taking place. The specific methods of warding off such dangerous drives or wishes are known as defense mechanisms. The operation of these mechanisms may result in a deletion or distortion of some aspect of *reality.* The following are examples of defense mechanisms and how they operate:

1) **Repression** — consists of the expelling and withholding from conscious awareness of an idea or feeling. It may operate either by excluding from awareness what was once experienced on a conscious level or it may curb ideas and feelings before they have reached consciousness, so that they never become conscious except as a result of analysis; thus a person can be unaware of feelings of hatred directed at a parent or sibling. Possible at any time during life, repression regularly occurs in respect to childhood events during the crucial period before six years of age (*infantile amnesia*).

2) **Displacement** — Repression may be bolstered and made secure by the investment of the repressed feelings in a substitute *object.* Thus a son who has repressed his hatred for his father may experience hostile feelings against other male authority figures.

3) **Reaction Formation** — also ensures the efficient maintenance of repression. It consists of the replacement in conscious awareness of a painful idea or feeling by its opposite. Thus a child who has repressed feelings of hate toward the mother may develop an extreme solicitousness and concern for her welfare.

4) **Projection** — is a process whereby a painful impulse or idea is attributed to the external world. The ideas or feelings which the person cannot tolerate in himself may undergo a transformation before they are projected, as in the case of *paranoid* projections which Freud recognized as being based on unconscious *homosexuality.* First, the feeling of love is transformed into hatred, and then the hatred projected onto the person who was the object of the unacceptable homosexual love. That person is then taken to be the persecutor, and the patient is the object of his hate.

5) **Isolation** — A splitting off of ideas from the feelings originally associated with them. Fleeting thoughts of an aggressive and objectionable nature—such as plunging a knife into someone, throwing a child out of a window, shouting obscenities in a public place—often occur without the emotion appropriate to such thoughts. The 'isolation' in such instances deprives the intent of the thought of its motivational force, so that action is thwarted and guilt avoided because the thought seems alien. Defense mechanisms may also function constructively in helping to make thought processes more efficient. Such use of isolation is illustrated in the dissociation of associated emotions from ideas in the process of carrying through a logical train of thought—to avoid contamination and distraction.

6) **Undoing** — Particularly in compulsive neuroses, a two-stage act may symbolically represent expression of an aggressive or sexual wish and its reversal or undoing. Some individuals habitually commit transgressions and try to undo them by expiations of various kinds, religious or self-punitive, for example.

Many defense mechanisms have been described. Aside from the six mentioned here, other important ones, *regression, introjection, identification,* and *denial* are discussed separately (q.v.). While the function of all these mechanisms is the same, i.e., to protect against painful feelings, they achieve this aim in different ways. For example, still another defense mechanism, **turning against the self,** does not ban the aggressive drive or impulse from consciousness as does repression; instead, it changes the object of the drive from another person to the *self*. It is operative especially in *depression* and *masochism* (q.v.). Defense mechanisms rarely operate singly; they occur together, combined into an ever varying mosaic, cooperating with one another in order to achieve the goal of excluding from awareness what is unacceptable. See *ego, ego functions.*

DENIAL: A defense mechanism of a primitive or early variety in which the *ego* avoids becoming aware of some painful aspect of *reality*. To bolster this effacement of a percept of reality, a fantasy is formed in the mind which erases the disagreeable and unwelcome fact. Thus a child who feels helpless and frightened may comfort himself with a *fantasy* of being powerful and omnipotent. Such a *defense mechanism* plays a normal role in childhood, but if it persists in the adult it results in severe illness, e.g. where in the face of a severe shock, like the death of a loved one, a delusion that the person is still living magically undoes the painful reality, and thereby denies the fact of death. Denial may persist normally, however, in the sphere of feelings or *affects* and as such may serve adaptive purposes. Thus we are all aware of the dangers of eruption of nuclear warfare but behave as though it could never happen, or we continue to travel in airplanes although crashes are not infrequent.

DEPERSONALIZATION: A disturbance in the sense of *self* (q.v.), usually experienced as a feeling of unfamiliarity in regard to one's own body or various of its parts. It is often reported by such phrases as 'I am surprised people recognize me'; 'I don't feel like myself'; 'I look at my hand and wonder to whom it belongs'. The basic content of depersonalization phenomena is that what should be familiar about the self is not.

DEPRESSION: This term is used to refer either to a specific mood or affect, or to a specific diagnostic classification.

The **depressive mood** is characterized by subjective feelings of sadness, lowered self-esteem, hopelessness, guilt, and diminished interest in outside activities. As a diagnostic category, depression includes both the subjective mood disturbance and specific objective phenomena. There is a marked slowing down of the vegetative processes, and a general lassitude prevails, with fatigue, anorexia (loss of appetite), constipation, and drowsiness with restless sleep, usually diminished but occasionally increased in amount. A frequent and very disturbing symptom is difficulty in thinking clearly or effectively.

In the agitated forms, there is overt evidence of *anxiety*. Drowsiness is replaced by insomnia, and overeating may replace the anorexia. Hypochondriacal anxieties become prominent and may be the main manifestation, or the presenting symptom.

Most of the mental content involves an increased concern with the *self,* resulting in a diminished interest in outside activities or people. Consistently present is the conviction that some part of the *self* is worthless or defective **(hypochondriasis)** or that some object or possession — spouse, child, dress, etc. —is 'no good', and must be eliminated. In the agitated form of depression, this narcissistic preoccupation includes fear of impoverishment, self-critical thoughts which may extend to suicidal ideation, and bodily anxieties.

Depression occurs as a reaction to the loss of an emotionally significant *object,* or of a personal ability or attribute. In that case, the individual reacts as if it were a loss from his own *self-image,* rather than the loss of an object. The self-criticisms, so characteristic of depression, can eventually be recognized as derived from criticisms originally directed towards an emotionally significant object, either the one lost, or an object connected with the loss in some way. The criticism itself is the expression of the anger that had been part of the original *ambivalent* attitude towards the object.

DEREALIZATION: A feeling that the outside world, which should be familiar, seems unfamilar and without emotional meaning. It is often reported by such phrases as, 'I know you are my mother, but you don't seem like my mother'. The world is sometimes experienced as colorless, gray, and drab. Not infrequently, derealization occurs in conjunction with feelings of *depersonalization* (q.v.). The experience should not be confused with boredom, apathy, or depressive lack of interest.

DEVELOPMENT: Refers to those growth processes and changes which are influenced by experience, and which arise out of the interaction of elements provided through maturation with the influences and attitudes from the environment: for example, the specific language learned by the child (English, French, etc.); specific defensive and adaptive modes and the correlated character traits; the specific familial-cultural value system internalized to form the *superego.* See *maturation.*

DISSOCIATION: May have a clinical meaning, or refer to the state of organization and activity of the *ego,* depending on the context. In common with psychiatric usage, as a descriptive clinical term, it refers to a state in which patients manifest confused thought processes and disorganized behavior, as for example in the *psychoses.* In a more restricted sense, it is used in psychoanalysis to refer to the fact that different *ego functions* (q.v.) in an individual may be at different levels of organization and adaptiveness. In a given person, some may be highly developed while others are regressed. This may be seen especially in the artist whose creative functions—his thought processes and his skills—are highly developed while his relations to other persons and his capacity to control impulses may be pathological. In this sense, we speak of dissociation of ego functions, and it follows that ego activity can be described only in terms of specific functions, and not in global terms.

DREAMS AND DREAMING: A universal and normal regressive phenomenon occurring during sleep in which thought processes and *affects* are represented in predominantly visual and (less frequently) auditory form. Other modes of sensory experience also occasionally participate in the dream, including touch, smell, and taste. It is a subjective experience, sometimes appearing banal superficially, but also often vivid and compelling. When associated with severe *anxiety,* the dream is described as a nightmare.

Dreams were originally described by Freud in *The Interpretation of Dreams,* one of the classical early works of psychoanalysis, as basically related to wish-fulfillment in their underlying or **latent content.** This understanding led Freud into some of his most important later concepts of psychoanalytic theory. Aspects other than wish fulfillment, such as mastery of infantile traumatic experiences, have been considered as additional psychological functions of the dream.

Dreaming, and the formation of dreams, is considered to occur through the **dream work,** a mental process characterized by archaic methods of thinking (see *primary process*), particularly displacement and condensation, which transform the latent dream thoughts into the **manifest dream.** Two other less significant elements of the dream work are **plastic** and **symbolic representation,** the transformation of the thoughts into sensory symbols and images (especially visual) and **secondary elaboration,** the linking together of the separate images and other elements of the dream into a relatively coherent story or action. In some instances, the latter does not occur, and the dream is recalled as a disjointed, incoherent or bizarre series of images or phrases. Dream work is the agency responsible for the distortion of the latent content into the peculiar form and appearance of the manifest dream.

The manifest dream content is the dream as it is recalled by the dreamer with its associated images, speech and sensory content as well as its specific **formal aspects** (including its division into parts, commentaries on the dream occurring within the dream, etc.). Dreams occurring within one night—or the same sleeping period—are considered to be part of the same latent thought sequence.

The process of **dream formation** is generally conceived as follows: Because of universal *regression* and the relaxation of conscious and unconscious censorship during sleep, there is a revival of an archaic form of functioning which is epitomized in the dream work (use of the *primary process* mode of thinking). The effect of the dream work on the derivatives of infantile drives, defenses, and their related conflicts as well as on their current representatives leads to the creation during sleep of predominantly visual images (the dream) to replace thought. A further step involved in dream formation is the contact between a **day residue** and the unconscious infantile drives and wishes of an erotic and aggressive nature. The resulting amalgam effectively disguises the infantile impulse which nevertheless remains the impetus for the dream. As mentioned above, to this disguise is added a process of distortion (including the secondary elaboration) accomplished by the dream work. The day residue is the dream's recent source material—elements from daily life which contribute to the formation of the dream. These events, impressions, perceptions, ideas and feelings from several days preceding the dream may in themselves be superficially trivial, but acquire their significance as dream instigators through their unconscious connections with the deeply repressed infantile conflicts or *instinctual drives* and wishes. The end result of this process occurring during sleep is the manifest dream.

It is now generally agreed, and confirmed by experimental evidence, that extensive dreaming occurs during every sleep. Dreams, however, are often not remembered, are forgotten, or are recalled only in very fragmentary form. This complete or partial exclusion of dreams from conscious awareness is related to partly (not well understood) physiological and partly psychological factors. The latter result from *repression* owing to *anxiety* or fears of social or moral disapproval of the ideas contained in them, or to unconscious **censorship** and *resistance*. Recall of forgotten dreams is often possible when the resistance is removed by analysis or by other means, such as hypnosis.

Dream screen is a term introduced by Bertram Lewin for a dream without recognizable or discrete visual content. It consists of a blank background, although it is not necessarily seen as such, or even mentioned by the dreamer. It is thought to be associated with infantile sleep and to be symbolically representative of the mother or breast. It may be the fulfillment of the wish to sleep, or of sleep itself. The dream screen is considered by some observers to be actually the background or matrix of the dream, and what appears on it, the visual contents, to be the waking elements.

Originally in *psychoanalysis,* dreams were considered by Freud to be the 'royal road to the unconscious'. With the increasing importance attributed to ego psychology and the associated structural concepts, work with dreams and their interpretation during analysis has become one of the several important elements in the *analytic process.* The therapeutic use of the dream thus refers to the utilization of the dream as an aid in the process of deciphering unconscious mental contents and integrating them into *consciousness,* both in terms of the infantile *fantasies,* drives, and conflicts and the defenses arrayed against them.

Recent experimental work on dreams and the dreamer, such as that of Charles Fisher and William Dement, is important but will not be discussed here.

DRIVES: These are motivational forces which initiate behavior. Freud conceived of two basic innate drives, sexual (libidinal) and aggressive, and referred to them as the *instinctual drives.* See *id, instincts,* and *instinctual drives.*

EGO: An important term in the history of the development of psychoanalytic theory, the ego has an early and a later meaning, both still used to some extent. Freud was at first somewhat vague concerning its meaning and employed it at times to refer to the total (mental) *self,* and at other times to an ill-defined portion of the conscious psyche (mind) as contrasted to the *unconscious,* both operating as mental systems to accomplish certain frequently antithetical goals. In modern usage, the term most often refers to Freud's redefinition of the ego in 1923 in *The Ego and the Id* (his statement of the *structural theory,* q.v.) as one of the three major functional subdivisions of the *mental apparatus.* Though it has some conscious components, many of the operations of the ego were then recognized to be automatic, unconscious mechanisms. One aspect of the ego in its earlier meaning has now been replaced by the concept of the *'self.'* In reading psychoanalytic literature, it is important to determine from the context the sense in which ego is used; this is often facilitated by noting the historical period to which the paper belongs.

In the structural sense of the word, the ego gradually evolves in the new-born infant from an undifferentiated psychic state. This ego-id matrix has a potentiality based on constitutional factors (the genetically determined growth pattern of the central nervous system, the special senses, and the body in general) and experiences in the surrounding world in relation to *objects.* The ego therefore occupies a position between the primal instincts, based on the physiological needs of the body, and the demands of the outer world; and as the internalized psychic representative of both, it serves to mediate between the individual and external *reality.* In so doing, it performs the important functions of perceiving the needs of the self, physical and psychic, and the qualities and attitudes of the environment (including objects); evaluating, coordinating, and integrating these *perceptions* so that internal demands can be adjusted to external requirements; and finally, in an executive way, bringing about relief from drive tensions and wishes through a discharge made possible either by reduction in the intensity of the drives (taming) or by a modification of the external situation to a degree realistically feasible. The important task of the ego, therefore, is to achieve optimum gratification of instinctual strivings, and at the same time to maintain good relations with the external world and the *superego* (the internal representative of the standards of behavior and moral demands imposed from without, and the threats consequent to failure to meet them). For this task, protective devices must be available to reduce excessively strong stimuli, both internal and external. Physiologically, the sense organs are equipped to select only certain stimuli and to reduce the intensity of others. This is especially important in infancy when other defenses have not yet developed adequately. (At that time the physiological mechanisms serving this purpose are referred to collectively as a protective shield or 'stimulus barrier'). Psychically, certain defensive functions are also developed and maintained to protect against conscious awareness of the demands of the *id* (primitive urges, impulses, biological needs, etc.) or *superego* that would be in conflict and give rise to intolerable anxiety..See *defense mechanisms.* In order to function effectively, it is also necessary that certain ego functions (e.g., *perception,* motor capacity, intention—anticipation, purpose, planning—intelligence, thinking, speech and language) mature relatively free of such conflict (a **primary autonomy** of the ego) or become conflict-free later **(sec-**

ondary autonomy). The *psychic energy* once devoted to such conflict becomes *neutralized* and thereafter available for the further development of the ego. As a part of its *adaptation* to *reality,* the ego must also develop the capacity for relatively stable relationships with *objects,* especially of the opposite sex, upon whom satisfaction of the instinctual needs of the individual depend. This involves the ability to form affectionate, friendly ties to other persons, with a minimum degree of expression of hostile feelings, and to maintain them over a long period of time (**object constancy**).

The ego should not be thought of as an anthropomorphic executor or as an actual part of the brain, but as a useful way of thinking about basic aspects of human behavior. It is best defined as a group of functions, which have a history in terms of early beginnings and subsequent growth, which are subject to numerous disturbances, and which may be altered in the direction of improved effectiveness in the course of psychiatric, and especially psychoanalytic treatment.

The specific functions of the ego are numerous, and there are few individuals indeed who achieve a high level of effectiveness in exercising them in most areas. Further, there are individuals who function very badly in some areas and with conspicuous success in others, as for instance, the ambitious, highpowered, successful executive who is incapable of giving his wife and children a reasonably happy life, or the dedicated and brilliant scholar who displays the most ludicrous ineptitude in the everyday affairs of life. There are, moreover, individuals whose disturbed ego makes it possible for them to achieve conspicuous success, such as the man whose intolerance to criticism makes him ride roughshod over all opposition, and the fanatical paranoiac who may sway millions with the fire of his delusional convictions. Adaptation to reality, which is the outstanding function of the ego, may take strange forms indeed. The ego must therefore be evaluated in terms of its specific functions, not as a totality.

See *adaptation, defense mechanisms, ego development, ego functions, psychic apparatus.*

EGO-ALIEN: Not in consonance with the *ego* in relation to *drives, affects,* ideas or behavior. The unacceptable mental contents are subjectively experienced by the observing ego as foreign to the *self*. Ego-alien is synonymous with **ego-dystonic,** the opposite of which is **ego-syntonic.** In these terms, ego is used in its earlier meaning, not the current structural one, to refer to what would now be called the self. However, **self-alien** or **self-dystonic,** though semantically logical, have not come into usage. For further clarification, refer to the definition and discussion of *ego*.

EGO AUTOMATISMS: Normal ego automatisms are *ego functions,* usually involving motor activity, which are conducted without conscious *attention* being directed to them. They have become *'preconscious'*, i.e., not conscious, but easily made so. In this category is the mastery of tasks such as learning to drive an automobile or to play a game such as tennis, mastering a foreign language, etc. In pathological automatisms, the actions are determined by unconscious needs and do not appropriately conform to the *reality* of the situation. They occur in psychotic states such as schizophrenia (e.g., monotonous repetition of the same phrase [**echolalia**] or repetition of what another person says) and in **fugue states** (altered states of consciousness during which an individual may go through elaborate patterns of action without being aware of it).

EGO DEFECT: 1) A developmental incapacity or impairment in the *ego* adversely affecting the whole development of *ego functions* but specifically those concerned with psychic defense and *adaptation*. 2) A developmental impairment of specific and major ego functions characterizing cases of *psychosis* in infancy and childhood, and also frequently found in adults with borderline or psychotic states.

EGO DEVELOPMENT: At birth the *psychic apparatus* is in an 'undifferentiated phase', which has the potentiality for *id* and ego development determined by hereditary and constitutional (innate) factors. What happens to the potential, however, depends greatly on the human beings surrounding the infant (the environment) and their capacity to love him for his own sake and not merely as an extension of themselves. In the course of ego development, certain events mark its growth and are reflected not only in external behavior but also in inner psychic states.

The infant is flooded by a mass of external stimuli of all varieties. Early in life these might be intolerable were it not for the **'stimulus barrier',** a physiologically less sensitive acuity to pain and other stimuli than exists in later life.

The primitive state of the ego also protects the infant from awareness of his helplessness and unpleasant stimuli of such intensity as to be unavoidable. The capacity to differentiate between pleasurable and painful states does exist, however, almost from the beginning, and a record of such experiences is registered in the form of **memory traces.** The *body image* is gradually built up by an amalgamation of these memory traces of sensations produced by stimuli, some from the physiological processes of the body and some from the ministrations of the first emotionally charged *object,* the mother. Psychic representations of other people are at first only partial, the breast, face, hands, and warmth of the body representing the mother. In the beginning, also, *self* and *object representations* are poorly differentiated, and even in adult life they remain somewhat fluid and interchangeable.

Gratification of physiological needs by the mother establishes memory traces of the satisfying experience which are reactivated in a wish-fulfilling way when, as inevitably happens, the mother is unable to satisfy them immediately. This progression from appreciation of need to the psychic state after satisfaction, even when the need has not been met **(hallucinatory wish-fulfillment),** has the anticipatory quality of a conditioned reflex, but it is also the beginning of *fantasy* and thought. The mother comes to recognize the meaning of her infant's motor activity and emotions, and her appreciation of and response to these preverbal signals establishes a primitive affecto-motor form of communication between them. The degree of satisfaction in this interchange probably contributes to the capacity for *empathy* in later life as well as to other character traits. In response to the smile of the mother, the infant smiles in return, and this imitation is the precursor of the later psychic process of *identification,* the basis of much ego development.

Repeated experiences of pleasure and pain are associated with human beings, especially the mother, but the child usually does not recognize her as an individual separate from himself until towards the end of the first year. At this time her absence brings discomfort (accompanied by **separation anxiety)** and the presence of strangers frightens him **(stranger anxiety).** These phenomena mark important stages of ego growth in the infant. Objects are beginning to appear as such, memories to be differentiated from current *perceptions,* and the precursors of defense against painful stimulation to develop. In its primitive functioning the ego follows the model of bodily functions: the mind introjects—i.e., takes in, as in nursing—what is need-satisfying and pleasurable, and it also seeks to deflect or ward off awareness of what is noxious or unpleasant or to eject, evacuate, externalize the impressions of such stimuli that have been unavoidably received.

From the latter half of the first year through the third, the child passes through a phase, described by Mahler as 'separation-individuation ', during which the psychic conception of the *self* is established as separate from that of the object. During the second year the infant moves in the direction of achieving the capacity to be alone. He no longer requires the constant presence of mother because she has, so to speak, grown into him and become a part of his personality, i.e., **object constancy** has achieved representation in his mind. This object constancy and mutually satisfactory *object relations* exert a powerful influence on ego development and vice versa. Even then satiation predisposes to fusion of self and *object representations* and return to a psychic state similar to the earlier unity with mother, while deprivation heightens the sense of separation. If the mother has not provided the infant with an optimal degree of instinctual gratification and frustration, graded to the needs and strengths of the child's developing mind, *individuation* and the development of a sense of *self* and *identity* are impaired. The very identity of the individual is therefore in part determined by the degree of gratification of instinctual needs he finds in relation to other people, mother and father most importantly in early life. The conflicts connected with such gratification may interfere with, or facilitate identification with the parent of the same sex. All individuals have some admixture of masculine and feminine qualities derived from identification with both parents.

In the early stages the infant cannot 'know' how helpless he is; his needs are satisfied as if by magic as other beings, not yet differentiated from himself, come and go; it is as if he were omnipotent. Later, when he becomes aware of his separateness and helplessness, he attributes this **omnipotence** to his parents and idealizes them. As he learns how dependent he is on those around him, he begins to crave their affection. He becomes willing to renounce certain satisfactions in return for being loved—a precursor of the ability to give as well as receive love passively. This marks the beginning of a change from passivity to activity—facilitated by the growing development of motor skills—by means of which he is ultimately able to attain some degree of mastery over his surroundings.

The development of speech in the middle of the second year and its maturation in the third to fifth years are accompanied by a great spurt forward in thought processes. '*Primary process*' thinking is replaced by '*secondary*,' but the latter remains fragile for a long time, magical thinking and omnipotence of thought continuing to exist in many situations. Through the psychic representations of object introjects, some control over impulses is achieved. However, the child still operates more through fear of actual punishment and the wish for the reward of love than through guilt and self-approval, which come only gradually, achieving their greatest development when oedipal wishes are renounced concurrent with an identification with the father (in the male child, formation of the *superego* as a result of resolution of the *oedipus complex*).

In this progressive development of ego functioning, differentation of the self from the object world has been succeeded by object constancy and finally, in adolescence, by the capacity for *object love*. For the latter, infantile objects and an extreme degree of self love (*narcissism*) must be relinquished. If the environment is suitably benign, *reality* is gradually mastered, objectivity in thinking occurs, autonomous activities increase in extent and power, and a reasonably efficient regulation of the *drives* is achieved. However, *maturation* of specific *ego functions* continues to occur until well into adult life as the individual develops a steadily increasing capacity to love, to work, and to adapt to the world about him.

See *active-passive, adaptation, character formation, defense mechanisms, development, ego, ego functions, maturation, psychic apparatus, psychosexual development, reality.*

EGO FUNCTIONS: The specific functions of the *ego* are numerous. In the definition given for the ego, they were categorized as perceptive, integrative, regulative, executive, defensive, autonomous, and object related. Under this heading will be discussed certain special ego functions which receive particular attention in psychiatry and psychoanalysis. To some extent they overlap.

1) **The relationship to reality.** This comprises not only **adaptation to reality,** requiring the functioning of the total person, mediated by the ego, but also what are called **reality testing** and the **sense of reality. Adaptation to reality** requires adjustment to alterations of the external world, whether it involves things, objects, or situations. There are individuals who find it very difficult to cope with changes in their normal routines, such as transfer to another position, an economic setback, an unfulfilled promise, etc. Some parents never become adjusted to the marriage or departure of grown children, and some children never, or with great difficulty, transfer their allegiance from their families to their spouses. **Reality testing** refers to the capacity to appraise correctly the external world and its generally accepted meanings. A conspicuous example of its failure is the *paranoid* delusion, which carries the conviction that neutral and innocuous people are determined to harm the person concerned. If a person only feels as if this were so but knows rationally that it cannot be true, reality testing is preserved despite severe emotional disturbance. In general, the preservation of reality testing distinguishes relatively normal and neurotic individuals from psychotic ones, although there are many instances in which the borderlines are blurred. The **sense of reality** is rarely disturbed except in very abnormal mental conditions, such as schizophrenia. In that case, the entire appearance of the outside world may seem changed—the sky may look dark and foreboding, buildings loom ominously; the person feels unreal, his body strange, with parts seemingly detached, etc. The sense of reality can, however, remain intact in the face of faulty reality testing, as in the case of brilliant paranoiacs who go about their daily business without any altered state of consciousness, but with delusions that are impervious to reason.

2) **Regulation and control of drives.** This ego function is manifested in the ability to withstand *anxiety,* frustration, *depression,* disappointment, postponement of expected satisfactions, etc., i.e., to hold in check and to distribute in a harmonious way the numerous demands for the expression of urges, needs and wishes that come from within. It implies the ability to wait, to delay satisfactions, not to be overcome by unexpected situations. It also implies the ability to suit the action to the intention, to find appropriate outlets for relief and satisfaction, and to engage in constructive, satisfying, and socially acceptable forms of activity (i.e., *sublimations,* q.v.).

3) **Object Relations.** There are two aspects to this ego function: a) The ability to form affectionate, friendly ties to other individuals, with a minimum of inappropriate feelings of hostility, and especially to have and to express feelings toward appropriate heterosexual objects. b) The ability to maintain such relationships consistently for a long time with a minimum of mutual interchanges of hostility. Disturbances in object relationships take the form of emotional coldness and detachment, inability to fall in love and to sustain love, self-centeredness, helpless dependency on others, or the necessity of dominating

them ruthlessly, and *perversions*. A childishly dependent person often tries to make his spouse behave like a parent rather than a marital partner. Sado-masochistic relationships (such as are portrayed in 'Who's Afraid Of Virginia Woolf?'), in which a marriage is carried on for years in a state of endless bickering, may bring morbid satisfactions to each partner. Perversions are characterized by varying degrees and types of abnormal object relationships or their almost total absence. The psychotic's relationship to objects is at such a faulty, primitive, and often—strangely enough—hypersensitive level, that one of his outstanding characteristics is the avoidance of human relationships.

4) **Thought Processes.** The ability to perceive what is going on around one and to coordinate, classify and 'make sense' of the perceptions; to think, to arrive at conclusions, to detect similarities and differences; to remember, to concentrate, to learn, to make judgments, to plan for the future—all these and other activities which we loosely call thinking, the ego function which distinguishes man from the lower animals, are also subject to far-reaching disturbances. Thus, with respect to mathematics and the physical sciences, Newton and Pascal were geniuses beyond measure, but in their beliefs and in their evaluation of human motives and behavior, their thinking was contaminated by serious pathological considerations. An individual is much more influenced in his appraisal of a political situation by his traditional background, his economic state and class, his prejudices and his personal animosities, than by cool and objective, impersonal considerations. Primitive people attribute human motives to non-human and inanimate objects and consequently live in a world of fear and superstition where consequences can be dealt with only by magical means. For ages man believed that disease was caused by demoniacal spirits or malevolent sorcerers, and it was not until men were capable of dissociating themselves from such faulty thinking dominated by fears and wishes that it was possible for progress to be made in conquering disease. Disturbances in thought processes brought about by masturbatory preoccupations in adolescence may result in disastrous consequences to the academic careers of many gifted children.

5) **Defensive Functions.** Historically, this was the earliest ego function defined by Freud; actually the one which initiated the beginnings of psychoanalytic theory was **repression.** Freud's ideas about the ego underwent marked changes, and his emphasis on its defensive functions varied over the years. At first he conceived of the ego as the conscious part of the personality, and defense, an attempt to ward off unacceptable sexual impulses and wishes, as a more or less conscious process; ultimately, however, the present concept of ego defenses evolved from the recognition that they, like the *instinctual drives,* operate at an unconscious level. Defenses are mechanisms employed by the ego to force out of awareness impulses, basically sexual and aggressive, which would arouse anxiety in the individual. Thus, the spinster who becomes enraged when she sees young people 'necking' in public is completely unaware of the fact that she is angry because she is sexually aroused by this sight, jealous of this free expression of sexuality, and threatened by an *impulse* which provokes *anxiety* in her. The ego, perceiving an impulse being aroused, experiences small amounts of anxiety in an anticipatory way and attempts to protect itself by instituting certain maneuvers, which we call 'defenses' or 'ego defenses'. Among the more important defense mechanisms are: intellectualization, rationalization, identification (used

as a defense, it most frequently takes the form of identification with an aggressor), introjection, projection, denial, repression, reaction formation, isolation, undoing, displacement, and regression. See *defense mechanisms.*

6) **Autonomous Functions.** Although most of the functions of the ego are easily affected by the instinctual impulses, so that their exercise can be seriously disturbed, there are a number of ego functions, termed autonomous, which are relatively resistant to such forces. These are perception, motility, (walking, use of the hands, etc.) intention (planning, anticipation, purpose), intelligence, thinking, speech and language. These 'primary' autonomous functions develop in the child at a certain pace, relatively more independent of the powerful forces of sexuality and aggressiveness than such functions as those described above (object relations, defenses, etc.). 'Secondary' autonomies are forms of behavior which begin as defenses against instinctual drives but become relatively free of such influences in the course of development. Thus, an individual, who rebels to an extreme degree against an authoritarian father to whom he unconsciously wishes to submit, may transform his rebelliousness into constructive social criticism. In the effective form his rebellion finally takes, it becomes emancipated from the passivity and reaction formation in which it was nourished.

7) **The synthetic, integrating, or organizing function.** This most important function refers to the capacity of the ego to unite, organize and bind together various drives, tendences, and functions within the personality, enabling the individual to feel, think and act in an organized and directed manner. This reveals itself in numerous individual experiences, which satisfy drives, ego interests, social demands, etc. in a harmonious way. It may also bring together various forces in a way, which while not completely adaptive to life, is the best possible one for the individual in his particular state. Thus, the formation of a symptom that represents the amalgamation of two opposing tendencies, while unpleasant, is preferable to yielding to a dangerous impulse or stifling it completely. An example of this is a *hysterical* conversion, which combines a forbidden wish and the punishment for it into a physical symptom. On examination, the latter turns out to be the only compromise possible under the circumstances.

EGO-IDEAL: The image of the *self* to which the individual aspires both consciously and unconsciously, and against which he measures himself. It is based on *identification* with the parents and other early environmental figures, as they actually are, were in the past, or as they have been idealized. To the extent that the actual self does not measure up to the ego ideal, the person's self-esteem suffers. The ego ideal is usually considered part of the *superego* (q.v.).

EGO IDENTITY: The experience of oneself as having continuity and sameness, especially in relation to the *ego's* synthesizing function. Also includes the individual's views, ideals and standards, his behavior and role in the society in which he lives. It is usually considered to be achieved developmentally during the normative crisis of adolescence. See *ego* and *identity*.

EMPATHY: A special mode of perceiving the psychological state or experiences of another person. It is an 'emotional knowing' of another human being rather than intellectual understanding. To empathize means temporarily to share, to experience the feelings of the other person. One partakes of the quality but not the quantity, the kind but not the degree of the feelings.

Empathy does not contain the elements of condolence, agreement, or pity essential for sympathy. One may participate in the joys and sorrows of another person in other vicarious experiences, for example, as in the theatre; but the aim is quite different. Imitation and mimicry also bear some resemblance to empathy, but they are conscious phenomena limited to the external behavioral characteristics of a person.

The capacity for empathy is an essential prerequisite for the psychoanalytic therapist. Usually a *preconscious* phenomenon, it can be consciously instigated or interrupted. It can also occur silently and automatically and may oscillate with other ways of relating to people. The essential psychic mechanism is the analyst's partial and temporary *identification* with the patient.

Both empathy and **intuition,** to which it is related, are means of obtaining quick and deep understanding. Empathy establishes close contact in terms of emotions and impulses; intuition does the same in the realm of ideas. Empathy is a function of the experiencing ego, while intuition seems to be a function of the observing ego. See *splitting of the ego*.

ENERGY, PSYCHIC: A hypothetical force in mental functioning considered analogous, but by no means equivalent, to the concept of energy used by physical science. Although conceivably not necessary, its use is intended to simplify and facilitate understanding of the observable facts of mental life.

This energy is considered to be derived mainly from the *instinctual drives* which impel the mind to activity; it serves as a source of the constant force operating in the transformations and vicissitudes of *libido* and *aggression*. Mental activity of whatever sort is accompanied by a transfer or flow of psychic energy (e.g. instinctual gratification results in its unimpeded discharge; thought processes result in only minimal discharge). While drives are the main source of psychic energy in the *mental apparatus*, energy from non-instinctual sources (also referred to as **primary ego energy**) has been postulated.

The amount of psychic energy invested in a mental process or representation is called its *cathexis;* the aspect of mental functioning which has to do with the amount of energy in any particular psychic phenomenon is called the **economic** (i.e. energic or quantitative) **aspect** of that phenomenon.

Psychic energy is postulated as varying in quantity (although it cannot be measured in any specific or physical terms), to be displaceable, and to exist in two states—one **free** or **mobile**, and the other, **bound** or **neutralized.**

Freely mobile mental energy accompanies the *primary process* and presses for immediate discharge, i.e., wishes of the system *unconscious* strive for immediate gratification. Energy which accompanies the *secondary process* is generally more or less bound, i.e., its discharge can be delayed temporarily or possibly indefinitely. Under the *topographic hypothesis*, the binding of psychic energy and the consequent delay in its discharge is characteristic of the functioning of the system *preconscious*. Under the *structural hypothesis*, the *id* is considered to work with free or mobile energy, while the *ego* works with relatively neutralized (i.e. de-instinctualized) energy.

Ego cathexis may be more or less mobile or bound. Mobility of cathexis is characteristic of ego functioning in infancy and early childhood as well as of those situations in later life in which *ego functions* are closely allied with id impulses and facilitate their discharge (e.g., sexual intercourse and orgasm). The capacity to bind psychic energy increases as the individual matures. It is closely related to the process and capacity for de-instinctualization or *neutralization*. The latter processes refer to the deflection of energy from its original pleasure-seeking aims and its utilization for ego functions which have no directly instinctual quality. Synonymous with **mental energy**. See *neutralization*.

EROGENOUS ZONES: Anatomical areas of the body which are biologically determined components of the sexual apparatus. The component *drives* are intimately connected to their respective zones, which become triggers of sexual excitation and discharge as peripheral extensions of the psychosexual organization. The zones are called erogenous because the craving for gratification connected with the sexual drive is related to them. The zones may be used for auto-erotic satisfaction, but are important organs of contact with the love object. The psycho-biological patterning and functioning of the erogenous zones have a profound influence on character development and symptom formation. Probably any area of the body (as well as the oral, anal and genital zones) may become secondarily invested as an erogenous zone. The psychosexual functioning of the erogenous zone is influenced by developmental and cultural factors. See *psychosexual development*.

EXTERNALIZATION: A term used to refer in general to the tendency to project into the external world one's instinctual wishes, conflicts, moods, and ways of thinking (cognitive styles). It is evident in young children who are afraid of monsters in the dark, in the savage for whom the jungle is populated by evil spirits, and in the paranoiac who sees persecutors all about him. The capacity for externalization may be used constructively in art, poetry, literature, etc. It is also the basis for the Rorschach test, which requires that an individual describe what he sees when he is presented with a series of standardized ink blots. The various shapes, forms, and movements he sees reflect various aspects of his personality, from which the examiner can make deductions about tendencies of which the person is unaware.

FAMILY ROMANCE: A generic term for varied *fantasies* which have two central themes, usually associated but also appearing separately. One theme enobles imagined instead of real parents, and the other involves a dramatic rescue in which the author may be the rescued victim but is more usually the hero.

Freud and Rank made the basic contributions to the understanding of the structure and meaning of the family romance. The essence of the first theme, according to Freud, consists of the child's rejection of his own parents, with the fantasy that he is the offspring of other parents who are generally of nobler lineage than his real ones. These new, exalted, and noble parents possess in the fantasy the identical idealized characteristics with which the child had endowed his own parents during his infantile period. The fantasy comes about as a result of the discrepancy between his idealized image and the real picture of his parents, stemming from the child's observations of defects in them. He is critical of them, dissatisfied with them, or feels slighted by them. Thus disillusionment stimulates fantasy that helps to make acceptable the separation and estrangement from parents which is a necessary step in *psychic development.* Another function of the family romance fantasy is to lessen oedipal guilt by denying the incestuous quality of libidinal feelings toward the parents.

In the rescue fantasy the individual imagines himself saving the life of some very important personage, a king, emperor, or other great man who is really a representative of a parent. In this way, Freud said, the child resolves his debt to his parents for having given him life. Oedipal wishes are in this instance dealt with by the defense mechanism of *reaction formation* (q.v.) at the same time that they are satisfied through placing the child in a superior, omnipotent position to be helpful to the displaced parental figure. Rank widened the scope of the family romance as described by Freud by associating it with rescue fantasies, relating both to the standard myth of the birth of the hero.

FANTASY: A product of mental activity which usually exists in the form of images or ideas. It represents an attempt at the fulfillment of a wish, and it is this wish-fulfilling quality which distinguishes fantasy from other mental products, such as ideas. Fantasies also have the quality of being *conscious* or *unconscious* depending upon their nature, origin, content, and ultimate fate. Conscious fantasies are often referred to colloquially as daydreams, and the wishes so fulfilled may be of an aggrandizing or sexual nature. As a rule, unconscious fantasies relate to important people in early life and express wishes that have a forbidden quality. Like any other mental product, fantasies may set in motion ideas or actions for the purpose of achieving satisfaction, or conversely may initiate various defensive maneuvers (e.g., repression, *denial*) to ward off the wish or its fulfillment if that would be a danger.

Certain common, if not universal, clusters of fantasies, which are concerned with important interests of early childhood, have come to be known by generic names, such as the *family romance fantasy,* the *oedipal fantasy,* the *beating fantasy*. In contrast to transient fantasies of topical nature, these basic fantasies exert an important influence in determining *character* and *symptom formation.* Those that are unconscious exert this influence by virtue of a psychic reality of their own, attributable to the lack of a conscious awareness which would permit their logical evaluation on the basis of external *reality*. Fantasy activity represents one form of thinking and so is a normal concomitant of the development of the *mental apparatus*. It serves, in children and adults, not only wish-fulfilling functions, but also preparation for realistic action appropriate to the requirements of the environment.

FETISHISM: A mental state which leads a person to worship or love a material object supposed to possess magical power or to be of special erotic interest. The fetish is a substitute for a deity or a beloved person, and a broad range of objects, varying in their characteristics, may be utilized for the devotional or loving behavior. In its religious context, the object may be an idol or other inanimate object that gains its power from the indwelling spirit, or it may be an object or body part of some revered spiritual leader. In its analytic context, the state of mind involved refers to the fixation of erotic interest on an object or body part which is inappropriate for normal sexual purposes but which is needed by the individual for the attainment of sexual gratification. These objects may be a part of the body such as hair, the hand or foot, or perhaps a shoe, handkerchief, or other object of personal apparel. The fetish usually symbolizes the female phallus, and its use represents part of a fantasy denying the danger of castration suggested by the anatomical difference between the sexes. See *splitting of the ego*.

FIXATION: The tendency in psychic development for residuals of earlier phases to acquire and retain strong 'charges' of *psychic energy,* and to play a significant role in later development of mental functioning. Arrests of development occur in both instinctual and *ego-superego* organization, permitting in various degrees the persistence of primitive ways of satisfaction, of relating to people, and of reacting defensively to old, even outmoded dangers. In addition to insufficiently known constitutional reasons for fixation (e.g.) inherent differences in the functioning of the various *erogenous zones,* and in ego 'givens'), there are inevitable experiences in which the developing, immature ego is overwhelmed by too much stress. These traumatic experiences usually involve an unfortunate combination of excessive satisfaction and excessive frustration. With disturbances of subsequent development and conflicts over contemporary functioning, *regression* is possible to these remnants of earlier functioning which are 'fixed' in the psyche. In his unconscious functioning, at least, the neurotic is 'pinned' or fixated to the past.

FREE ASSOCIATION: The method of thinking and reporting of the patient which is used as the basic procedure in *psychoanalysis.* The patient is asked to let his thoughts flow freely and to say everything that comes to mind without the selectiveness ordinarily dictated by social conventions. The type of thinking involved is similar to the thought processes engaged in while driving, shaving, or in other semi-automatic tasks; the thoughts move freely from one topic to another, oscillating between fantasy and reality, without ever losing sight of reality entirely and occasionally sharply focusing on it. The difficulties in freely associating, common to almost everyone in the beginning, such as blocking, evasion, and a disturbing discontinuity, become an important subject of analytic *interpretation* itself. These are '*resistances*' which reflect the unconscious defenses employed to avoid awareness of disturbing material.

In the *analytic process* an observing function of the *ego* is encouraged. This is accomplished by the frequent focusing of *attention* and logical thought on the nature and meaning of the products of free association. Some patients have considerable difficulty in letting their thoughts roam freely, while others may succeed quite well in that task but not be able to achieve sufficient objectivity to observe the trend and meaning of associations, even with the help of the analyst. The ability to engage in both processes constitutes an important criterion for analyzability.

FRIGIDITY: A lack of responsivity of a woman during the sexual act with a man. There may be varying degrees, ranging from total lack of erotic physical sensation to full participation and enjoyment of the sexual act with the apparent sole exception of ability to achieve orgasm through coition. Intermediate gradations include inadequate vaginal transudation (the fluid lubricating the vagina) and the absence of psychic excitement and pleasure even when the involuntary contractions of orgasm occur. Anatomical and hormonal factors as well as unconscious psychic processes accompanying the stages of female *psychosexual development* are individual bases for frigidity. The sexual partner, inadequacy of stimulation, and the social and cultural conditions under which intercourse takes place are other important determinants.

GENITAL PHASE: The final stage of *psychosexual development.* It begins with puberty and the biological capacity for orgasm. At this time the component sexual drives, derived from earlier stages of psychosexual development have been organized in the service of ultimate genital satisfaction, although they are still utilized for sexual excitation in foreplay. The genitals have primary importance, however, and at orgasm discharge the tension that may have been elicited initially in the non-genital activity. The term implies more than a physiological capacity for orgasm, which may occur with *masturbation* or *perverted* acts. Also involved are attitudes and feelings which connote non-narcissistic *object love,* the capacity for true intimacy, and the security for flexible *ego regression.* Such a level of personality maturity is possible only after successful resolution of the conflicts of the oedipal phase and adolescence.

HOMOSEXUALITY: Is manifested by the overt or latent disposition to sexual desires and excitement directed towards members of the same sex, with concomitant lack of sexual arousal and desire, or even aversion in relation to the opposite sex. The primary characteristic of homosexuality is a deviation in the choice of the sexual object. In contrast to the formerly held view that innate, hereditary factors lead to homosexuality, it is now considered to be a disturbance of the total *psychosexual development,* especially during the oedipal phase.

In the **male homosexual** there is, as a rule, an overly strong attachment to the mother up to and including the oedipal phase, which is not resolved by *identification* with the father but rather by partial identification with the mother. *Object choice* is narcissistic in type, i.e., the loved person must be like the self, and sexual excitation is experienced in regard to men instead of women. Due to strong castration fears the homosexual man cannot tolerate a sexual partner without the tremendously valued male organ. Another common motive for homosexual object choice is the avoidance of rivalry with father and brothers.

In **female homosexuality (Lesbianism),** the woman retains the strong original pre-oedipal attachment to the mother, which is displaced onto the homosexual partner. As a result of an unsatisfactory outcome of oedipal conflicts, her identification with mother is incomplete and she holds on to mother as an object of love.

Latent or **unconscious homosexuality** is encountered in normal heterosexual individuals to a greater or lesser degree. Usually, homosexually directed *libido* is diverted from the physical relation to socially accepted objectives (*sublimation*) or spent in the service of an admired person or cause (bound by the *ego ideal*). If these measures are not successful, and the tendency is so strong as to threaten to become overt, severe *anxiety* or other symptoms may result.

HYPNAGOGIC PHENOMENA: Consist in the appearance of visual imagery when falling asleep. Similar sensations may be experienced when waking up and are then called **hypnapompic phenomena.** As in dreams, ideas and concepts may be represented by sensory images in these experiences. The **Isakower phenomena** may be considered special instances of hypnagogic imagery but, as a rule, are not limited to visual images alone. Hypnagogic phenomena occur more frequently in childhood and adolescence and diminish in frequency in adulthood. They should be distinguished from hallucinations, similar in nature but not related to sleep, which indicate more serious psychopathology.

HYSTERIA: A *psychoneurosis*—often referred to as conversion hysteria, to differentiate it from *anxiety hysteria*—characterized clinically by 1) conversion symptoms and 2) an apparent affective indifference to the disturbance ('la belle indifférence'). Occasionally, either separately or together with the foregoing, there are episodic states or major 'hysterical spells', characterized by the *dissociation* of mental functions, (e.g. double or multiple personalities, fugue states, somnambulism, major *amnesias,* etc.).

Conversion symptoms are physical manifestations not caused by or related to anatomical or physiological pathology. Among these are symptoms derived from motor, sensory or visceral reactions—anesthesias, pains, paralyses, tremors, deafness, blindness, vomiting, hiccoughing, etc. However, hysterical patients are often convinced their symptoms are due to objective physical disease, although their affective reactions are inappropriate to such conviction.

These syndromes are unique in every individual, and analysis demonstrates that they are historically determined by specific repressed experiences in the individual's past. They represent an expression in 'body language' of specific unconscious *fantasies,* developing as a compromise in the conflict between an instinctual wish which has given rise to *anxiety* and the defense against that wish. Hysterical spells are often pantomimic expressions of complicated fantasy stories which can be analyzed in the same way as the elements of the manifest *dream,* since both phenomena are products of the distortion resulting from mechanisms utilizing *primary process.*

Hysterical symptoms occur when there is difficulty at the level of resolution of the **oedipal conflict.** Here the wish for the incestuous love object represents the chief danger. The major defenses used are **repression** and *regression,* leading to dissociated bodily and affective symptomatology that acts as a distorted substitute and compromise for the original infantile sexual gratification. The choice of *symptom* (including affected organ or body zone) is predominantly based on the content of the unconscious fantasy and the ability of the organ to symbolize the unconscious forces involved. These symptoms are thus, par excellence, an example of the 'return of the repressed'; both the instinctual wish and the defense against it are re-enacted in the symptom. The ensuing suffering or deprivation represents the *masochistic* punishment for the partial gratification of the forbidden fantasy.

The conflict arising from the constellation of oedipal wishes and fantasies and their opposing defenses may not be converted into bodily symptoms. Instead, it may contribute to a distortion in *character formation.* The resulting **hysterical character** is histrionically exhibitionistic, labile in mood, and prone to act out his oedipal fantasies with persons on whom his parental feelings are displaced.

In general, psychoanalytic treatment offers a good to excellent prognosis for this neurosis.

ID: A totally unconscious part of the *mental apparatus* which represents the sum total of most 'wishes' arising from the individual's needs, which in turn are indicated by their 'mental representations', that is, the *instinctual drives.* This implies that the instinctual drives are the essential 'components' of the structure id. However, it has been suggested that the id represents a broader concept than its most important component, the *instinctual drives,* and particularly more than its formulation as a 'chaotic cauldron' of mobile energy. The id may be considered to be the result of interaction between innate and environmental factors, and to include the sum total of 'wishes' which are the resultant of certain *perceptions* and memories of the earlier gratification of basic physiological needs. See *structural theory, psychic apparatus.*

IDENTIFICATION: An automatic, unconscious mental process whereby an individual becomes like another person in one or several aspects. It is a natural accompaniment of maturation and mental development and aids in the learning process (including the learning of speech and language), as well as in the acquisition of interests, ideals, mannerisms, etc. An individual's adaptive and defensive reaction patterns are often attributable to identification with either loved and admired persons, or feared ones. By means of identification with a needed person an individual can often provide for himself the satisfaction of the needs desired from that person. Separation from a loved person becomes more tolerable as a result of identification with him.

For identification to occur, sufficient psychic development must have taken place for the individual to distinguish himself from others in his environment. Such differentiation of *self* and *object representations* normally occurs in early childhood.

IDENTITY: The experience of the *self* as a unique coherent entity which is continuous and remains the same despite inner psychic and outside environmental changes. The **sense of identity** begins with the child's awareness that he exists as an individual in a world with outer objects, and that he has his own wishes, thoughts, and memories, and his own distinctive appearance. *Identification* with both parents gives a bisexual quality to *self-representations* in children of both sexes. Eventually, however, an integrated self-representation (*self-image*) is created out of the multiple former identifications contributing to character traits. In respect to sexual identity, that self-image usually represents a predominant identification with the parent of the same sex. Relative stability of the sense of identity is achieved with the resolution of bi-sexual identifications and the completion of adolescence. The sense of identity is the self-image as perceived by one's self and entails awareness of some, though not all, physical sensations, emotional feelings, and character traits. **Personality,** on the other hand, is the impression perceived by others of the individual's physical appearance, affective expressions, modes of speech, and behavior.

IMPULSE: The sudden, unpremeditated welling up of an *instinctual drive* toward some action, which usually has the quality of hastiness and lack of deliberation. The term is applied either to psychic awareness of the desire to act or to the action itself. Morbid impulses are further characterized by an irresistible and impelling quality in a setting of extreme tension where expression may be inappropriate. The impulse may be sudden and transitory, or the associated tension may rise to a crescendo leading finally to uncontrolled expression (e.g. an exhibitionistic act). Frequently there is explosive and violent action with disregard for others and, at times, for the subject himself.

The disturbances of impulse observed in a wide variety of so-called '*impulse disorders*' (q.v.) have certain characteristics in common: 1) There is an understandable quality about the impulse. Distortion of sexual and aggressive wishes is not as marked as in classical neurotic symptoms. Usually its meaning is quite apparent to the observer, who empathically realizes that it is the kind of phenomenon he could give expression to himself under comparable conditions. As a general rule, it is wholly or partly in harmony with the momentary aims of the psyche. Morbid impulses may be felt in the same way that common impulses are felt by 'normal' people. The morbidity is attributable to the irresistible quality, the manner in which the impulse is expressed, or the fact that it is expressed in an unsuitable setting. 2) The impulse has a pleasurable component at the moment of expression even though the individual may criticize and despise himself for it. Sometimes horror is felt that he enjoys the act, which is experienced as happening against his will. See *acting out, impulse disorders.*

IMPULSE DISORDERS: A heterogeneous psychopathological group characterized by disturbances in impulse control. Addictions, *perversions,* impulse neuroses, kleptomania, impulsive psychopathic characters (i.e. *character disorders*) and even accident-proneness and fate neuroses are among the various clinical syndromes included in this group.

What these various conditions have in common is that the impulsive behavior, not consciously perceived as abnormal, is both pleasurable and irresistible. It results from impairment of those normal *ego functions* which delay, modify and otherwise control the expression in behavior of primitive impulses. The relative loss of control permits discharge of original, usually repressed, impulses in a minimally distorted fashion. In general, individuals suffering from these conditions are fixated at *pregenital* and preverbal stages of development; they have little tolerance for drive frustration as a result of *identification* with parental objects who provided inadequate models for the development of *superego* standards and prohibitions, and ego controls.

Disorders of impulse control vary widely in symptomatology, *psychodynamics,* and genetic development and therefore do not constitute a distinctive special group of clinical conditions; however, they are frequently considered together because of the particular characteristics which they share in common.

INCORPORATION: A special form of *introjection*, a taking into the mind of the attributes of another person, which follows the model of the bodily function of oral ingestion and swallowing. It is the primary mechanism in *identification* (q.v.), the process whereby change in individuality is accomplished through becoming like someone (or something) else. Identification accomplished via incorporation implies change by fantasied oral consumption of an *object* (person), as indicated by cannibalistic wishes in dreams and associations. The mechanism is encountered in *psychoses, impulse disorders,* severe oral characters, and in less neurotic individuals during states of severe *regression* in analysis. Although it has some import for psychological understanding (being one way of mentally assimilating interpretations), it is a hazardous basis for mental stability since such incorporative identificatory mechanisms may malfunction or break down easily.

INDICATIONS FOR ANALYSIS: The particular clinical features of a patient with a predominantly psychological illness which suggest the use of psychoanalysis as the treatment of choice. These include not only the specific elements of the symptomatology and the pattern of illness, but also the relevant aspects of the patient's basic personality (i.e. *character structure*), his life situation, and the realistic considerations which bear on the possibility of obtaining and utilizing such treatment.

Generally, analysis is considered to be indicated when there is a neurotic or psychosomatic illness of such severity (resulting in major intellectual, social and emotional, or even physical disability and suffering) as to warrant an intensive and extensive therapy. An evaluation of the patient's motivation, adaptability, relative freedom from possible disruptions, and the capacity to follow the basic rules of analysis (*free association,* regular attendance, the non-withholding of information, etc.) should indicate these factors as sufficiently strong and stable to lead to the expectation of a favorable result. The factor of so-called ego strength (which includes the attempted assessment of a significant number of the more important ego functions) is usually considered to be of major importance in the analyst's decision; certainly there should be adequate ego functioning to permit at least partial cooperation with the fundamental rules. Many, but not all, cases of psychosis are considered unanalyzable by most analysts for this reason.

Recently there has been a trend toward the use of analysis in psychological illness previously thought to be inaccessible to this technique. This often requires the use of *parameters*. This trend has been epitomized in the phrase, 'the widening scope of psychoanalysis'.

INDIVIDUATION: The maturational and developmental processes that occur from the latter half of the first year through the third year of life (separation-individuation phase), in which the intrapsychic representations of the self and the love object, the mother, are gradually differentiated. It is sometimes compared to a second birth experience, a 'hatching from the symbiotic mother-child common membrane'. An important step in the development of the sense of reality occurs when the mother-child omnipotent unity is relinquished. Psychotic disorders in childhood may be precipitated when predisposed children are faced with this step in development.

INFANTILE NEUROSIS: The psychological symptomatic manifestation of the universal developmental conflict taking place at the *phallic-oedipal phase* of development. Freud introduced the term to describe the stresses and disturbances that he considered to be the common fate of all human beings when they pass through this stage of development. It is a concept that has occupied a central position in psychoanalytic thinking, especially since emotional health or neurotic disturbances in childhood or adult life depend on the appropriate resolution of the *oedipus complex* and the infantile neurosis.

The roots of infantile neurosis, with its potential for healthy or pathological developments depending on its solution, appear developmentally in early infancy and are further influenced during the unfolding developmental sequences. The various *pre-oedipal phases* and, most important, the *oedipal complex* itself contribute to the formation of the infantile neurosis. Some children who have had difficulties (usually resulting in *fixations*) at the earlier *oral* and *anal phases* experience the phallic-oedipal phase as very threatening and anxiety-provoking, which then may cause a *regression* to one of the earlier phases. External and internal conflicts as well as defensive reactions result in transitory or persistent neurotic symptoms (among these are *anxiety* and panic attacks, physical symptoms, feeding and bowel disturbances, inhibitions, *phobias,* magical rituals and *obsessions,* etc.).

Unlike the adult, whose neuroses may or may not show a close correspondence to his infantile neurosis, and who often experiences his disturbance as **ego-dystonic** (i.e. like a painful foreign body), the child's neurosis is usually more disruptive or disturbing to his family or school than to the child.

INFANTILE SEXUALITY: The sexual *drive* is a normal and universal phenomenon which appears in infancy and undergoes a phasic maturation subject to developmental influences. The satisfaction of basic bodily needs, such as hunger or excretion, is accompanied by pleasurable sensations which become an end in themselves. Gratification of these needs by the mother (or mother substitute) introduces an erotic quality, which eventually becomes object-directed, through the stimulation of the affected zones (oral, anal, phallic) of the body.

During the **oral phase** (approximately until 18 months), the major site of tension and gratification is the mouth, lips and tongue; in the next 18 months the anus and surrounding area takes over as the leading zone. During the latter period, erotic pleasure is achieved both through the function of excretion and its eventual mastery, mediated again by the crucial relationship with the child's most important *love object,* the mother. (See *anality*). The pleasurable sensations accompanying the passage of urine contribute to **urethral erotism.** while concurrently, exhibiting and looking acquire a libidinal aspect. During the third year, the genital begins to assume the leading sexual role, at first for both sexes primarily in terms of the easily visible male organ.(See *phallic phase*). However, the stage of adult sexual organization, the *genital phase,* does not occur until puberty when the capacity for orgasm is acquired.

The earlier sexual stages each make their own important contribution to the final organization of sexual drives in the adult. These are often referred to as **component (partial) drives.**

Another important characteristic of infantile sexuality concerns the relationship of the child to the objects of his sexual longing. If the child cannot have the love object (mother) or the **part-object** (breast) that he wants, he may gratify himself on his own body (thumb-sucking, etc.). This capacity to gratify his sexual needs on himself is known as **autoerotism**, and any erogenous zone may be utilized. This differs from the *narcissism* which develops somewhat later essentially by being without external object involvement. The narcissistic phase develops when the infant takes his own body (*self*) as a love object.

A still later and extremely important phase, considered generally as the climax of infantile sexuality (and followed by the *latency period*), is the **oedipal phase,** when object-related fantasies are usually expressed through genital masturbation. The special form of the *oedipus complex* varies for the individual child dependent on constitution and experience, but the universal characteristics are embodied in the oversimplified phrases: 'love for the parent of the opposite sex' and 'death wishes against the parent of the same sex'. See *oedipus complex.* It is apparent from the foregoing that in psychoanalytic usage 'infantile' refers to the entire period of early childhood up to *latency* (about six years of age).

When the adult genital organization has been achieved with genital discharge of sexual excitement, infantile sexuality is still regularly manifest in fore-play (touching, kissing, sucking, masturbatory play, etc.). Infantile sexual maturation is concurrent normally with a progressive taming of the aggressive drive, with increasing control over instinctual expression, and a growing love and tenderness for the loved object.

Infantile sexuality is relatively unintegrated compared with adult genitality; this concept is often expressed by the description of the infantile zones and modes of gratification as being **polymorphously perverse.**

INSIGHT: The subjective experiential knowledge acquired during psychoanalysis of previously unconscious pathogenic content and conflict. Analytic insight differs from other cognitive understanding in that it cannot occur without being preceded by dynamic changes leading to the weakening of resistances and the release of energies. These augment the autonomous *ego functions* which make insight possible. Among the more important autonomous ego functions involved are self observation, synthesis, perception, memory and reality testing, control over regression and affective discharge, and integration.

Pseudo-insight may occur in which there is apparent intellectual understanding of the forces involved, but instead of an integrative, energy-releasing function, the knowledge serves a libidinal or aggressive purpose in respect to the analyst, e.g. to please and to deceive and defeat him.

INSTINCTS: A term introduced by biologists, mainly students of animal behavior, which has been widely applied to the behavior of man. The broadest definition of instinct is that of a species-specific behavior pattern, based mainly on those potentialities determined by heredity ('innate givens') and therefore considered to be relatively independent of learning. The term was applied earlier to a great variety of behavior patterns (e.g., maternal instinct, nesting instinct, the instinct of seasonal migration of birds, etc.) defying, especially at the time this concept reached the height of its popularity, any physiological explanation. However, it also had a strong teleological connotation, conveying the meaning of purposefulness, as in the concept of the instinct of 'self preservation' which played a major role in earlier hypotheses. The latter concept was frequently used by Freud until about 1932, but its validity has been questioned even by such strong proponents of the instinct concept as the group of students of animal behavior called ethologists (e.g., Lorenz, Timbergen, and others). The reason is simple. Present theories of evolution and of genetics hold that evolutionary change takes place mainly through mutations. Those mutations which have a greater survival value for the individual species are transmitted by the genetic code and result eventually in the preponderance of bearers of those particular qualities achieved by the mutation. This is in accord with Darwin's concept of 'natural selection'. As a result of this fact, as well as the refinement of behavioral and physiological proofs of learning, most biologists, and especially such American students of animal behavior as T. C. Schneirla, rightly criticize the instinct concept. They prefer to speak simply of species-typical behavior patterns; these are of course based on innate equipment, but such patterns mature and develop through a certain degree of interaction with the environment.

While the term 'Instinct' was originally used in psychoanalysis to express the concept dealing with the motivational forces of human behavior, today these forces are usually subsumed under the concept of *instinctual drives* (q.v. for definition and discussion).

INSTINCTUAL DRIVES: Freud's concept of a motivational force of human behavior was, since the beginning of his theoretical formulations, one of the cornerstones of psychoanalytic theory. He used for this concept the German word 'Trieb'. Before dealing extensively with various explanations and applications of this concept, Freud offered several definitions. His most cogent one was '. . . an instinct . . . appears to us as a concept on the frontier between the mental and the somatic, as the psychical representative of the stimuli originating from within the organism and reaching the mind, as a measure of the demand made upon the mind for work in consequence of its connection with the body'.

This definition shows that Freud's concept of 'Trieb' is really a biological as well as a psychological one. Psychoanalysts vary in the emphasis they place on the biological or the psychological aspect. However, it has to be kept in mind that all such concepts are meant to be explanatory constructs. Such concepts as *drive, psychic energy,* etc. are not meant to express something as well defined and quantifiable as physical or chemical energy.

Freud's definition refers to the psychic representation of internal stimuli. These stimuli represent physiological needs. Hunger, for example, illustrates the difference between such physiological processes as lowering of the blood sugar level, emptying of the stomach, etc. and what eventually becomes the 'psychic representation' (which may be *conscious, preconscious* or *unconscious*) of these physiological manifestations. What Freud had in mind when he spoke of 'Trieb' was the sum total of such mental representations of the various somatic needs. (As will be seen, this explanation will be important for our understanding of the concept *Id.*)

Unfortunately the word 'Trieb', which Freud used for his concept, has usually been translated, especially by Strachey in his otherwise masterful *Standard Edition,* into 'Instinct'. The fallacy of this and the resulting confusion in the usage of this term is explained in the definition of the term *'instinct'*. The instinct concept of biologists and students of behavior conceptualizes a behavior pattern and also includes the assumption of the motivational force which induces a special type of behavior, while Freud's concept 'Trieb' tries to conceptualize only the motivational force.

We might ask why Freud's semantic formulation 'Trieb' was not simply translated as 'Drive'. The reluctance to do this was based on the following reasons: 1) The drive concept has been greatly abused in the behavioral sciences, and also in certain biological studies. The number of motivational forces called 'drives' is growing constantly; 2) Freud assumed that 'Triebe' are based on innate givens, which are, as pre-formed potentials, present at birth. This was one of the reasons why Strachey, and others before him, chose the term 'instinct' as a translation. The term 'instinctual drives' expresses then, in its first word, an emphasis on the evolutional aspect of the concept 'Trieb', and avoids, on the other hand, the semantic pitfalls of the word 'instinct'. It is for these reasons that Hartmann, Rapaport, and Schur, among others, have urged persistently the use of this term, and suggested that the term 'instinct' be used only when we intend something analagous to the instinct concept of biology.

Freud attempted to conceptualize his theory of instinctual drives in different ways, trying first to find a general, all-encompassing term, and eventually arriving at his final formulation. It distinguishes between 'Libido' or 'Eros' and 'Aggression', which he formulated in terms of what he called the 'Death Instinct'. Freud's concept of libido or eros is to be understood as the most general term for the much narrower term of sexuality. It encompasses all the processes, both physiological and psychological, which strive for synthesis, as well as all the positive aspects of human relationships and the factors which enter into the motivation of most human activities.

Freud's concept of the death instinct is his most controversial one and has been severely criticized both within and without the psychoanalytic field. Most psychoanalysts assume that this formulation is a highly speculative one, which thus far cannot be confirmed by any biological investigation. However, Freud's writings show his recognition that the death instinct can be observed only in aggressive, destructive actions directed either towards the environment or turned against one's own person. Most psychoanalysts therefore use, both in their clinical approach and in their writings, the concepts of the **libidinal** and **aggressive** instinctual drives.

INTELLECTUALIZATION: The psychological binding of the instinctual drives in intellectual activities, especially as a measure of control. This is exemplified by typical adolescent preoccupations with philosophy and religion. Under favorable circumstances, these trends may enrich knowledge and the intelligence, but pathological distortions create typical symptoms of obsessive and paranoid thought. Not infrequently, intellectualization is used during the course of psychoanalytic treatment as a resistance against achieving emotional insight.

INTERNALIZATION: In its broadest aspect, a progressive process by which external interactions between the organism and the outer world are replaced by inner representations of these interactions and their end results. In an evolutionary sense, the *mental apparatus* and its physical substrata (including the *instinctual drives*) are structural records of the experiences of the race, substituting inner for outer controls and thereby serving the purposes of self-preservation and propagation of the species. Through their influence on *superego* formation, social institutions may be considered elements in a biological frame of reference. Psychologically, memory (with symbol formation) and the anticipatory and decisional aspects of thought constitute the vehicles of internalization. *Incorporation, introjection* and *identification* are object-related mechanisms used for this purpose; **projection** and action are correlated externalizing processes.

INTERPRETATION: A form of intervention by the analyst, whose aim is to achieve therapeutic results by adding to the patient's knowledge of himself through making him aware of psychic content and conflict which had been warded off. In general, interpretations are dynamic or genetic in nature. Dynamic interpretations refer to psychic forces operating to produce a particular effect on mental life at any given time. Genetic interpretations are concerned with indicating or clarifying the connections between past mental states and present ones. (*Reconstruction* may be considered as a special form of genetic interpretation, but is not identical. We reconstruct events, but we interpret meanings.)

INTERVENTION: Any communication from analyst to patient during the analytic hour. A generic term which includes explanations, confrontations, questions, clarifications, *interpretations* and *reconstructions.*

INTROJECTION: Originally used synonymously with the term *identification.* Recently it has been differentiated from identification and employed in two different contexts:

1) The assimilation of the object-representation into the self-representation whenever the boundaries between the self and object representations are indistinct. The individual then becomes confused in regard to his separateness and even his *identity.*

2) The child's taking into himself as a psychic phenomenon the object's (usually parent's) demands as if they were his own, so that he reacts in the same way whether or not the object is present. The child does not copy the object as he would if he identified with it. The regulating, forbidding and rewarding aspects of the *superego* are formed by the introjection of parental directions, admonitions and rewards.

LATENCY: The state of relative inactivity of the sexual drive during the period from the resolution of the *oedipus complex* to pubescence (from 5-6 years to 11-13 years). Sometimes used to refer to the *latency period* itself, as in 'latency-age boy'. At this time subsidence of infantile sexual activity is followed by a major displacement of drive energy into socially approved channels (primarily learning). In most societies it is coterminous with the period of education in basic cultural skills, and it is thus a period of considerable ego development and differentiation.

LIBIDO: A quantitative concept which refers to a measure of the drive energy of the sexual instinct. It does not denote either sexual appetite or conscious sexual desire. Currently it is used to represent sexual drive energy, and does not refer to the energy of the aggressive drive. Libido was recognized early by Freud as one great dynamic force which gives rise to internal conflict in the course of mental development; the other major forces were the self-preserving interests of the individual and the aggressive drives. The libido can cathect (i.e. be invested in) the intrapsychic representation of objects (*object libido*) or the self (*narcissism*).

LIBIDO THEORY: The theoretical description of a characteristic biological maturational sequence of libidinal phases from the *oral to the* mature *genital* phase. (See *infantile sexuality.*) The theory assumes that the sources of the sexual instinct are derived from complicated somatic processes which exert a continuous demand upon the *mental apparatus,* an influence which is psychologically experienced as an impulse. There are **component drives,** usually associated with specific *erogenous zones* and phases (mentioned above), and typical wishes or *fantasies.* The drive organization is subject to progression, *regression* and *fixation;* it is normally organized under genital primacy after puberty. A latency period is postulated between infantile sexuality and post-pubertal genitality.

Freud's discovery of the significance of sexual desires in the formation of neurotic and psychotic symptoms necessitated an extensive exploration of the origin, development, and vicissitudes of sexual drive influences from birth to old age. The study of these phenomena is called libido theory. The libido theory dominated psychoanalytic thinking and concept formation from Freud's first discoveries of unconscious motivations until the early 1920's, at which period the ego and its development began to share the interest of psychoanalytic psychology. However, as an explanatory principle, the libido theory remains indispensable in psychoanalytic theory and practice, interrelating sexual drive organization with total personality development.

MASOCHISM: A propensity to seek physical or mental suffering in order to achieve, consciously or not, sexual arousal and gratification in the widest sense. 1) **Sexual masochism** appears early in childhood, usually coupled with sadism, as a 'partial drive'. (See *infantile sexuality.*) Remnants of it persist in adult life as an attenuated component in forepleasure in many normal people, more often in women than in men. 2) **Masochistic perversion** is a condition in which sexual gratification is contingent upon physical or mental pain, such as beatings, threats, humiliations, imagined or actually experienced at the hands of the partner. 3) In **moral masochism** an unconscious or conscious need for punishment leads to symptoms, such as anxiety states, or to unconsciously self-inflicted suffering. These manifestations can be shown to appear as a consequence of situations which normally would lead to satisfaction, rise of self-esteem, or happiness. This condition may lead to a type of therapeutic failure, known as *negative therapeutic reaction.* 4) **Masochistic character,** or **behavioral masochism,** has in common with moral masochism that the sexual arousal and gratification bound up with suffering are unconscious. It differs from moral masochism by a prevalence of depressive moods, and a tendency to complain about being the victim of the unfairness and malevolence of people and fate. Whereas moral masochism and behavioral masochism are mainly based upon an unconscious regressive sexualization of guilt feelings, the pathogenesis of masochistic perversion is based, in men, on unconscious passive homosexual tendencies; in both women and men, on the particular form and means of undoing childhood fears of castration, of rejection, and of abandonment by the parents.

MASTURBATION: Refers to volitional, genitally directed, rhythmic self stimulation which produces sexual pleasure. During infancy, non-specific, random exploratory behavior, which may include the genitals, has been called **infantile masturbation** by some observers but genital play by others. Such genital play is one of the various types of **autoerotic** activity of infancy, and it may be considered an indicator, at that age, of satisfactory relations with the environment. Conscious or unconscious *fantasies*, which always accompany infantile and later masturbation, contribute to personality development and evolving *object relations*. A necessary and logical development of genital play, masturbation during childhood and adolescence is therefore to be considered normal. This may be true also in adult life if it is a substitute outlet for the sexual drive when no sexual object has been available for a period of time. In analysis, it is not masturbatory activity itself which is the focus of attention, but rather the fantasies accompanying it and their effect on personality development.

Any organ which can produce sexual pleasure may be utilized for masturbation. Secondary *erogenous zones* may become the focus of sexual excitation and the site of precursors of *perversions*.

When fantasies are sufficiently intense to produce a complete discharge of sexual excitation without physical contact, it is described as **psychic masturbation.** Masturbation may also be masked, the sexual excitement persisting, but neither the activity nor its sexual character being recognized as such. This may become associated with non-sexual activity such as gambling, flying, dangerous games, or reckless driving. In addition to the struggle against the act of masturbation, which leads to **masturbation equivalents** (nail biting, scratching, head banging), there may also be a struggle against the associated fantasies. The fantasy becomes unconscious and displaced onto certain *ego* activities. The behavior pattern may then express masturbation fantasies and take the form of quarrelsomeness, criminal activity, exaggerated interest in anxiety-provoking events, compulsive talking, and other obsessional symptoms. Compulsive masturbation may have various origins in which the discharge sought may be non-sexual (rage) as well as sexual. It may not only serve to achieve sexual pleasure, or relieve guilt, but also to diminish anxious excitation, or to revive a traumatic excitation from the past.

MATURATION: The process involving those 'intrinsic factors' (i.e. biologically determined) in the growth and differentiation of the personality which are prior to and relatively independent of experience. Thus, maturation refers to the unfolding of phylogenetically evolved and, therefore, inborn apparatuses and functions. These emerge in the course of embryonic development or are carried forward after birth as Anlagen which become manifest at later stages in life. Conversely, *development* refers to the emergence of structures, functions and behavior which are the outcome of exchanges between the organism and the inner and outer environment. Examples of maturational processes (occurring in a normal child in an average expectable environment): the gradual attainment of full physical size; the attainment of adult sexual capacities as a result of the endocrine charges of puberty; the endowment of the various ego apparatuses such as those relating to motor activity, speech and language. Also see *development*.

MELANCHOLIA: The original term for *depression* (q.v.) now rarely used. It refers to depression as a diagnostic category only, and not to the depressive mood or *affect*.

MENTAL APPARATUS: Synonymous with *psychic apparatus* (q.v.).

METAPSYCHOLOGY: A term first used by Freud to indicate that the assumptions of psychoanalytic psychology went beyond the scope of conscious experience to explain behavior. It represents the highest level of abstraction in the continuum from clinical observation to psychoanalytic theory, and serves as a conceptual tool for establishing an orienting and systematizing framework around which clinical data and lower-level psychoanalytic propositions can be organized. Since the academic psychology of the late 19th and early 20th century equated 'mental' with 'conscious', unconscious processes were considered outside the realm of the mind and hence 'beyond psychology' (the literal translation of metapsychology).

A metapsychological explanation of behavior includes dynamic, economic, and structural viewpoints, with the more recent addition of genetic and adaptive aspects. The **dynamic** point of view concerns itself with the psychological forces involved in behavior, and in particular with the clash or conflict between instinctual drives and restraining influences in the past and present. The **economic** point of view is concerned with the deployment of psychological energies, and the increases or decreases of such energies. The **structural** point of view consists of those assumptions concerning the organized, enduring psychological configurations subsumed under *ego, superego* and *id*. This includes, among others, character traits, defenses, habits, moral standards, attitudes, interests, memories, ideals, etc. Through identificatory processes, these are the precipitates of early *object relationships*. Structures are distinguished from forces in that they persist in time and have a slow rate of change while forces constantly change in magnitude and direction or disappear when discharged.

The **genetic** point of view refers to the history of the drive processes and ego functioning, which express themselves in a given behavior, as well as the history of the subject's relation to the situation in which the behavior occurs. The **adaptive** point of view considers the intrapsychic changes and the modifications of the environment achievable through the ego's activity, necessary to bring about a harmonious relationship between instinctual drive forces, internalized restraints, and the requirements of the external world.

NARCISSISM: A concentration of psychological interest upon the *self.* This may range from healthy self-esteem and normal concern about oneself to pathological forms of brooding, and to such severe degrees of self-preoccupation as that of the schizophrenic who stares at his image in the mirror or fantasies constantly about himself. Under normal circumstances, people's interests are divided between a concern for themselves (narcissism) and for the world of things and people around them (*object love*). Painful self-consciousness, and an increased propensity for shame, are the outcome of conflicts over narcissism. On the other hand, pride and pleasure in one's own body and mind, one's achievements, and in that part of the surroundings which the individual regards as his own, such as his family, his nation, and his possessions, may be regarded as manifestations of a healthy self-esteem. Injury to one's narcissism (e.g., blows to one's self-esteem) tends to evoke severe degrees of anger, often referred to as narcissistic rage.

NEGATIVE THERAPEUTIC REACTION: A specific clinical response which occurs during the course of certain analyses. This response, a seemingly paradoxical one, suggests a worsening of the patient's condition which, however, follows closely upon a period of what ordinarily would be regarded as effective therapeutic management. Such a negative reaction originates in a variety of possible determinants. Typically, it may be encountered in masochistic patients with strong unconscious needs to suffer and endure punishment; often these needs had previously been gratified in the discomforts of the neurosis itself. However, when effective analytic work, with the obvious expectation of symptom relief, threatens to upset the delicate balance previously established, it must be met masochistically with increased suffering through a flare-up of symptoms. See *masochism.*

NEUROSIS: Originally the designation for the functional physiological disturbance (mediated by the autonomic nervous system and the neuro-endocrines) accompanying strong affective feelings, principally anxiety. It is now used loosely but almost universally as synonymous with psychoneurosis, its psychological counterpart. See *'actual neurosis', anxiety, psychoneurosis.*

NEUTRALIZATION: A hypothetical psychic process whereby free ('unbound') instinctual energy, aggressive and libidinal, becomes modified and 'tamed'. *Sublimation* is now considered to be one example of the more general process of neutralization. The process of neutralization is significantly linked to the normal development of psychic structures—the *ego* and *superego.* Hence it has been proposed that a failure in this process would account for the impairment and defective development of the ego and superego in *borderline states* and schizophrenia.

OBJECT CHOICE: The conscious choice of a loved person, influenced strongly by unconscious determinants, and offering gratification of certain *instinctual drive* demands. This selection may represent the choice of an individual who shares similar qualities with a loved object who offered gratification in infancy or childhood. Object choice has been further characterized as: *narcissistic* and anaclitic. In the former instance, an individual may choose someone who is like himself (embodying some characteristic of his own personality) or what he would like himself to be. An **anaclitic object choice** refers to a choice based on the unconscious wish to receive passive gratification, i.e., to be symbolically fed and protected as the individual was by an object (usually the mother) at an earlier time. All of these determinants are often present in the unconscious choice of a loved person.

OBJECT LIBIDO: The energy of the sexual drive which is directed toward external loved objects (persons). Object libido is therefore sharply contrasted with narcissistic libido (the libidinal *cathexis* invested in the *self*). See *libido*.

OBJECT LOSS: 1) The actual loss of a loved person through separation, illness or death. 2) It may also refer to the experience of loss of love in the subject's inner world without the actual occurrence of the real loss or threat of loss of a loved person.

Thus, the fundamentally *ambivalent* instinctual attitude of a child toward his parents may lead him to experience (often by means of **projection)** a threat of loss of love. Also the individual's relationship to external objects may be repeated within the *ego* itself. For example, the experience of loss of love in depressive illness may have little to do with the patient's actual relationship with external love objects, but may reflect instead the reaction imposed by an extremely harsh *superego*. The experience of object loss may also result from a change in the internal psychic state as in a narcissistic *regression*.

OBJECT LOVE: The type of love relationship with another person which occurs when that individual is cathected (invested) with *libido*. Originally, libido was invested in the *self*. Part of this narcissistic libido may be detached and transformed into object love. If such object love is based on the resemblance of certain attributes of the object to real or wished-for aspects of the self, it is said to be narcissistic in type.

OBJECT RELATIONS: Relationships taken in their broadest sense to include not only relations where there are direct instinctual gratifications (both libidinal and aggressive), but also relations where instinctual gratification is *sublimated,* as occurs in friendships and the love between parent and child. It is generally agreed that the capacity to love is a function that assumes increasing importance during normal maturation and development. There are individuals whose egos have been distorted or arrested in development and who evidence a stunted and immature capacity for object relations; this is characteristic of *borderline* and *psychotic* individuals. These more primitive forms of object relations have been described as *transitional object* relations and also as *symbiotic* object relations. Primitive object relations, in contrast to more mature forms of *object love,* are characterized by a relative inability to maintain the love relationship in the face of frustration and to accept the limitations and separateness of the loved object. Thus the child's attachment to his parents may be bonds of love, of hate, or of both (i.e. *ambivalence*), the last being by far the most usual.

To describe the process simply, *identification* of the child with the mother, existing from an early stage, gradually develops into an object relationship. The mother, as the first love object, is the object most highly cathected in the child's world, and the child's earliest learning proceeds partly by identifying with this object. An indication of the major importance of progressive object relations in optimal functioning is the positive correlation between the development of the *ego* and the child's *object relations.*

OBJECT RELATIONSHIPS: See *Object Relations.* The terms are used interchangeably in psychoanalytic writings, although object relationship may sometimes refer to a specific instance, type or quality of *cathexis* of a person or his representation with *object libido.*

OBJECT REPRESENTATION: An enduring schema of a particular person other than the *self* modelled by the *ego* from a multitude of impressions, images and experiences with that person. A person recognized only because of his capacity to gratify instinctual needs is referred to as a **need-satisfying object.** Object representation comes to exist when the schema exists, independent of such need satisfaction. For example, after the construction of the representation of the mother, the child perceives her as one and the same person even when he does not require her services (i.e. when she is sleeping, talking, walking, eating, etc.). Together with the self representation it provides the material and framework for all mentation including the *ego's adaptive* and *defensive functions.*

OBJECT WORLD: The representation of external objects in the inner world of the subject's mind. They may correspond to actual experiences but are often altered by *fantasy*. Some authors contrast the various representations of loved objects with the representations of the *self* and refer to a 'self and object world.'

OBSESSIONS: Any thought including wishes, temptations, impulses, reflections, doubts, commands or prohibitions can be designated as an obsession when it intrudes repeatedly and involuntarily on the subject's consciousness.

Obsessions are related to and usually combined with various *compulsions*. While the former are persistent, unwelcome morbid ideas, compulsions are persistent and irresistible tendencies to engage in apparently meaningless motor acts. In both symptoms the afflicted person usually has some degree of insight into the pathological or morbid nature of the process, but is unable to control it.

OBSESSIONAL NEUROSIS: (Also known as obsessive-compulsive neurosis; infrequently called psychasthenia.) A type of *psychoneurosis*, (or in Freud's original description, one of the *transference neuroses*) characterized by obsessional thoughts and compulsive acts. See *obsessions* and *compulsions*. In addition, rumination, doubting and irrational fears are often present. All of these are accompanied by morbid *anxiety* when the intruding thoughts or repetitive acts are prohibited or otherwise interfered with.

The clinical picture of obsessional neurosis results from both a libidinal regression to the **anal-sadistic phase,** (usually because of severe conflict during the **oedipal phase**) and the ego's defensive activities which here include the mechanisms of **isolation, reaction formation** and **undoing.** Other major characteristics underlying the symptomatology are *ambivalence,* a regression to magical thinking, and indications of rigid and destructive *superego* functioning. The *conflicts* usually involved in this neurosis are closer to those of the prephallic phase of *psycho-sexual development* than to those of the phallic-oedipal period.

OEDIPUS COMPLEX: A characteristic grouping of *instinctual drives,* aims, *object relations* and fears universally found at the height of the *phallic phase* (3-6 years). During this period the child strives in a limited way for sexual union with the parent of the opposite sex and the death or disappearance of the parent of the same sex. Co-existing with these strivings, but usually less prominent, is the negative form of the complex; in this case the child wishes for sexual union with the parent of the same sex, and the death of the parent of the opposite sex. The specific **talion** (retaliatory) **fear** for these forbidden incestuous and hostile wishes is that of castration in the male, and injury to the genital and procreative organs in the female. Genetically (see *metapsychology*), it is a nodal point crucial to the further growth and development of the immature *psychic apparatus;* through its resolution it contributes to the coalescence and definitive formation of the *superego. Topographically,* the complex is usually partly conscious and evident in speech, behavior and other modes of communication during childhood. In later life, it is most often unconscious, but dependent on the extent of resolution, it is more or less evident in behavior, attitudes and *object choice,* and has an important bearing on *character structure,* the nature of *object relationships* and sexual *identity, fantasy* formation and later sexual patterns and activities.

Together with the *unconscious* and *infantile sexuality,* the *oedipus* complex is one of Freud's greatest discoveries, made during his self-analysis in 1897. He was struggling with the inconsistencies of his earlier 'adult-seduction-of-children theory' of neurosis and with his doubts about the new science. Under the pressure of recognition of hysterical symptoms in his family and himself, he entered into a period of intensive introspection, including his dreams, which he called his self-analysis. In a famous letter to Wilhelm Fleiss, dated October 15, 1897, Freud stated his finding: "I have found love of mother and jealousy of the father in my case too, and now believe it to be a general phenomenon of early childhood. Every member . . . was once a budding Oedipus". He had discovered infantile sexuality and the oedipus complex in himself, and tentatively assumed its universality. In presenting this thesis for the first time in *The Interpretation of Dreams,* Freud used his own dreams and those of others to correlate the myth of Oedipus with the unconscious wishes of every man.

The classic **Oedipal myth** tells that Laius, King of Thebes, was warned by an oracle that a son yet to be born would kill him. When Jocasta, the queen, gave birth to a boy, the king ordered that the infant be exposed to die on a mountain side with his ankles pierced and bound. A shepherd of Corinth found the infant and brought him to King Polybus, who adopted the boy and raised him as his own son. In young manhood he left Corinth for reasons which vary according to different stages in the development of the myth. All agree, however, that Oedipus chanced to meet Laius at a cross-roads and in a quarrel about the right-of-way slew the king, his father.

As Oedipus traveled on, he came to the Sphinx who blocked the road to Thebes and challenged every traveller to answer a riddle or die. Oedipus mastered this riddle of life, and the Sphinx jumped to her death in mortification. The grateful Thebans made Oedipus king and married him to Jocasta. However, the gods would not tolerate incest, even without conscious participation, and a plague fell upon Thebes. According to the oracle, finding the murderer of Laius was the price for lifting the plague. As the Sophocles play unfolds, Oedipus, sworn to uncover the crime and thus save his city, finds he is the murderer, married to his own mother. In the tragic ending, Jocasta hangs herself and Oedipus blinds himself with the brooch used to fasten her dress.

There are many conceptual phrases derived from the oedipus complex, which require some clarification.

The **oedipal phase** is considered by some authors to be identical with the *phallic phase* of development (2½-6 years) while others reserve the term for that period toward the end of the phallic phase when the oedipal complex is well formed structurally and dynamically.

Oedipal conflict is a term that refers to various conflicts characteristic of the Oedipus Complex (q.v.). The urge for sexual union (id oriented) is in conflict with *castration anxiety* (ego and superego oriented). There are, moreover, the antithetical positive and negative phases of the complex, active and passive aims of the drives, masculine and feminine *identifications* in the fantasy of sexual union. One level of conflict can intensify another; for example, *castration anxiety* as fear of retaliation from the father may be superimposed on castration anxiety as a result of a wish to be feminine with father and receive a baby from him.

Oedipal triumph is that circumstance in which the child has gained the major love and attention of the parent of the opposite sex with devaluation or elimination of the parent of the same sex, e.g., when the mother is the aggressive member of the family and adores her son, while she demonstrates contempt for the masculinity of her husband. Another frequent circumstance is the death of the parent of the same sex during the person's childhood. Many authors, especially Ernest Jones in *Hamlet and Oedipus,* stress the tragic and fateful consequences of the gratification of this repressed and consciously unacceptable wish.

The **oedipal situation** is a loose reference to a conglomerate of the phase, conflict, and complex, specific for the psychic development of a particular person, as evidenced in the masturbatory fantasy and *family romance* of that person. It is also used to refer to a current life situation in which fantasies, feelings, and behavior derived from the oedipal phase are reawakened. See *infantile sexuality, psychosexual development, phallic phase.*

ORALITY: A comprehensive term which designates all those psychic interests, mechanisms and inclinations (as well as their manifestations) that stem from the early libidinal and aggressive functions of the oral cavity.

In the early stages of life the infant's needs, perceptions and modes of expression are mainly centered in the mouth, the lips, the tongue, the pharynx and the upper digestive tract. These convey the sensations of thirst and hunger, the pleasurable tactile stimulations evoked by the nipple or its substitutes, the sensations involved in the act of swallowing and the feeling of fullness. The infant's earliest feelings of pleasure and manifestations of *aggression* originate in this area, referred to as the **oral zone**, and contribute to its outstanding importance in psychic development.

Throughout approximately the first eighteen months of life the **oral zone** maintains its dominant role in the organization of the psyche, leading to the designation of this period as the **oral phase** of libidinal development. Subsequently, with the ascendancy of the other erotogenic zones (anal and then genital), this role becomes proportionately less, although its effects on personality development remain profound throughout life.

The states of psychic excitation and tension caused by the oral zone's libidinal and aggressive needs are conceptualized as being the outgrowth of specific psychic forces, the **oral drives**. These consist of two separate components; one directed towards the satisfaction of the libidinal needs, and the other to the satisfaction of the aggressive needs. These states of oral tension lead to actions directed towards assuaging them, and their subsidence is referred to as **oral satisfaction** or **oral gratification**. A typical example of such gratification is the condition of quiescence reached by the infant at the end of the nursing situation. This state is characterized by the **oral triad**; it consists of the wish to eat, to sleep, and to reach that feeling of relaxation, yielding and falling which occurs at the end of the act of sucking just before the onset of sleep. The latter wish is the original nucleus of ideas of being enveloped and devoured. These may present themselves later in life in *fantasies, anxieties, phobias,* and manifestations of the Isakower phenomenon, which, if displaced, may become a part of the *castration complex.*

While the libidinal needs (pleasurable sucking) are prominent in the earlier stages of the oral phase, the aggressive ones tend to emerge later, particularly after the eruption of teeth, and constitute the psychological basis for **oral aggression** (also called **oral sadism**). This is the part of the oral drives motivated by the **aggressive instinct** which expresses itself in chewing, biting, and spitting; it may also play an important role in such conditions as *depressions,* addictions and *perversions* later in life.

When oral drives are blocked by psychic forces (defenses) which interfere with their emergence, a state of **oral conflict** ensues. This may manifest itself in multifarious symptoms, such as a general distaste for food, specific food idiosyncrasies, vomiting, spasm of the jaw, grinding of the teeth at night, speech. inhibitions, etc. Oral conflicts and early life vicissitudes in the area of orality (especially excessive indulgence or severe deprivation), in addition to causing symptoms such as those just mentioned, may also manifest themselves in a number of specific character traits and abnormalities. When some of these traits —including, among others, excessive optimism or pessimism, greed, demandingness, excessive generosity or penuriousness, dependency, restlessness, impatience, and curiosity—acquire a dominant importance in an individual's total makeup, we speak of an **oral character structure**, which may present itself in a large number of possible constellations.

OVERDETERMINATION: The causation or production of a specific symptom, item of behavior, or any element of psychic life, by a variable number of intersecting causal paths. A particular phrase or thought from a patient may be determined simultaneously by the meaning he is consciously conveying, by his *transference* feelings, by certain *drive* derivatives or by defensive operation of the *ego,* etc. An image in a *dream* may be determined by a number of different 'intersecting' lines of **latent thought content**, while *symptoms* have many layers of meaning to the patient, including gratification of wishes, the need for punishment, as well as various secondary gains.

The term is derived from geometry; two intersecting lines determine a point; three lines intersecting at a point overdetermine the point. However, in psychoanalytic usage the term implies several lines but does not necessarily imply more than necessary, so that the term **multidetermination**. sometimes used synonymously, is preferable to overdetermination.

PARAMETER: A psychoanalytic parameter is a term relating to an aspect of psychoanalytic technique. It conceptualizes departures from a hypothetical baseline, namely, the classical analytic technique in which *interpretation* is the exclusive technical tool. A typical parameter is the advice given to some phobic patients to expose themselves to the allegedly dangerous **phobic situation**. A parameter should be introduced only when it is likely that 1) without its introduction the *psychoanalytic process* would come to a standstill; 2) it will not make a return to standard technique impossible; 3) it becomes dispensable after fulfilling its usefulness; 4) the patient can gain *insight* into its function.

PARANOID: An adjectival term referring to psychopathological conditions characterized by strongly held ideas or delusions of persecution, jealousy, and grandeur (i.e. **megalomania**). Closely associated terms are: paranoia, paranoid psychosis or schizophrenia, paranoid character, and paranoid condition.

True **paranoia** is a relatively rare condition, a *psychosis* developing relatively late in life; its existence as a separate disease entity has been questioned. Its features are somewhat intermediate between those of the paranoid condition and paranoid schizophrenia (i.e. paraphrenia). The paranoiac, whose thought processes and other *ego functions* are generally well preserved, experiences highly systematized delusions of persecution, usually involving the state (especially the police or military), the church, his employer, or his family. Grandiose ideas may include the belief that the individual is an inventor, the founder of new religious or political systems, a great lover, or a member of royalty. Hallucinations are quite rare in this syndrome. Particularly in persecutory ideas (delusions), there is often a 'kernel of truth' at their core (some *unconscious perception* or empathic understanding of the other person's equally unconscious *affects* or wishes). The 'truth' may also relate to observations of events during childhood that were denied at the time. These elements later return to *consciousness* distorted and magnified in an irrational, delusional form.

On the basis of his psychoanalytic study of the Schreber case, Freud suggested that delusions of persecution, of erotic potency, and of jealousy represent a defense against unacceptable homosexual impulses. Stated simply, the idea 'I love him', based on the homosexual wish, is changed by **reaction formation** to 'I hate him'. Still unacceptable in this form, the feeling related to the second statement is projected, so that it corresponds to 'He hates me and is persecuting me.' Later, understanding of the aggressive drive led to the inclusion in the formulation of the wish to destroy the loved and hated object. In addition to the strong *superego* reaction against homosexual and aggressive strivings, other important factors that contribute to the underlying character structure and etiology (cause) of paranoid conditions are major tendencies, especially *narcissism* and *passivity*.

Paranoid condition usually refers to a pathological state lying between paranoia and **paranoid schizophrenia.**

Paranoid character is the term applicable to an individual whose personality structure is dominated by marked suspiciousness, querulousness, and persistent rationalized hostility against other persons or groups. The use of scapegoats or 'enemies', the need to 'defend' against a hostile world (representing *externalized* aggressive impulses within the individual himself), the tendency to fight excessively over minor causes (often becoming litigious), and frequent contempt for others are the traits usually observed in this disturbance. Here the characteristic and most frequently observed defense mechanism is **projection**—the **displacement** of the individual's unacceptable wishes and thoughts on to others, who then are felt to direct these ideas back to their source (i.e. I hate him; no, he hates me, and therefore I am justified in attacking and beating him). This permits the rationalization of the individual's hostility, and allows him to defend his megalomanic image and *fantasies*. In spite of their pathology, however, certain paranoid characters have contributed some of the basic systematic research in science, as well as classic works in art, music, and literature.

PARAPRAXES: Faulty acts or blunders, as in slips of the tongue or pen, or lapses in memory. Freud demonstrated in 1901 in *The Psychopathology of Everyday Life* that these seemingly meaningless errors are, in fact, symptomatic acts determined by *unconscious* motives. This extension of the concept of *psychic determinism* has become commonplace and today the 'Freudian slip' is part of our idiom.

PENIS ENVY: A mental attitude and feeling of discontent with one's own genital equipment, together with an aggressive urge to possess the genital apparatus and to identify with, and take over, the imagined superior achievements and potency of the male. Frequently found in women, the attitude is associated with unconscious (sometimes partially conscious) fantasies in which the male genitals are over-valued and associated with omnipotence. Accompanying the discontent is an unconscious belief in the universal possession of the penis at birth. Its absence in the female is explained by the *fantasy* that it was lost due to the neglect or evil intent of the parents (usually the mother), or as a punishment for the misconduct of the little girl, usually for *masturbation.*

This state of envy may refer to 1) a developmental stage in girls most prominent from three to five years of age (the *phallic phase,* q.v.); 2) an unconscious fantasy, usually weakly cathected in women whose infantile *conflicts* about sex have been successfully resolved; 3) a more or less unconscious and pathological constellation in neurosis. In the latter case penis envy is frequently involved in *symptom formation.* The symptoms are a compromise, expressing simultaneously the wish to castrate the male and take away his penis, and an identification with the male by means of a fantasy which denies the penisless state by displacing the over-valuation of the penis to her body, a part of her body, or an attribute, such as intelligence (the 'illusory phallus'). Penis envy often leads to intense rivalry with men and manifest sexual dysfunction at all levels, including *frigidity* and *homosexuality.*

Breast envy, a male counterpart to penis envy, may be one of the consequences in boys and men of the 'small penis complex', which is also a derivative of *castration anxiety.* Through its equation of the breast with the penis, breast envy may represent one aspect of the *unconscious fantasy* of a phallic woman, serving to deny the danger of castration suggested by the observation of the penis-less state of the female. While such fantasies are ubiquitous, they play a specific and major role in the *psychodynamics* and pathology of the *perversions.*

PERCEPTION: One of the essential, innate functions of the *psychic apparatus,* based on the biologically determined potential of the brain and nervous system. It has a neuro-physiologic substratum involving neuro-receptors or sensory 'end-organs', nerve pathways, and areas of central registration in the brain. The sensations so received from stimuli are translated into psychological equivalents. If a sufficient charge of *psychic energy* (*attention cathexis*) is attracted to the sensory percept, it may attain the quality of *consciousness,* but many percepts are registered, stored in memory, and utilized without conscious awareness. Though transient in nature, perceptions supply information about the outside world which, as memory traces, are used to build a store of memories serving other ego functions. Thus they are essential for **reality testing** and the evaluation of qualities of other people with whom *object relations* are established. There is a close connection between cognition and perception, which provides the stimulus for the operation of the ego function of thinking.

Disturbances of perception may arise from neuro-physiologic causes or from psychological sources. In the latter case, if perception becomes involved in *conflict,* the external percept may be denied or distorted, its memory trace **repressed,** or its significance dealt with by other *defense mechanisms* (q.v.). The effect of *intrapsychic conflict* and the operation of defenses against perception may be observed in the differing testimony of witnesses of an emotionally charged event.

The new-born infant is presumed to have a **protective shield** (the *Standard Edition* translation of what was previously called the **stimulus-barrier**)—a relative lack of perceptual acuity due to its undeveloped nervous system and *mental apparatus*—which protects it from being flooded to an overwhelming degree with unpleasant stimuli that would be indiscriminately registered.

PERVERSIONS: A variety of sexual practices that deviate in aim or object choice from the accepted norm of heterosexual genital union. A true perversion implies an habitual (although not necessarily exclusive) type of behavior. This should be distinguished from the occasional type of sexual act performed by people, usually during foreplay, whose conduct otherwise falls within the accepted norm. In a true perversion the deviant behavior is persistent, and is more important to the individual than is heterosexual genital intercourse. The perversions represent the persistence into adult life of infantile or **polymorphous-perverse** sexual activity. (See *infantile sexuality*). Among the more common perversions are: *homosexuality;* painful acts to provide sadistic or masochistic pleasure; oral-genital contact (fellatio, cunnilingus) as the primary gratification, rather than as excitation preliminary to intercourse; **sodomy** (intercourse through anus or with animals); **pedophilia** (sexual acts with children), etc.

PHALLIC PHASE: The stage in *psychosexual development* (approximately from 3 to 5 years of age) which succeeds, and to some extent overlaps the *anal phase* of libidinal organization. It is characterized by a primarily genital focus of sexual interest, stimulation, and excitement. The penis (phallus) becomes the organ of principal interest to children of both sexes, and the anatomical configuration of the female genitalia is considered as evidence of castration. Actually the little girl's organ of sexual excitement during this period is the clitoris, which is embryologically the homologue of the penis. However, its relatively hidden position and its minimal erectile capacity make for a markedly unsatisfactory comparison with the boy's erectile and highly visible phallus.

The phallic phase is also associated with the probably universal practice of genital *masturbation,* accompanied by predominantly unconscious *fantasies* of sexual activities (as understood by the child) with the *love objects,* the parents. The awareness and frequent visual experience of the penis-less mother or little girl ushers in an intense preoccupation with *castration anxiety,* often connected with fears or actual threats of punishment for *masturbation.* It also leads into the opening phases and reactions of the *oedipus complex.* In little girls, the awareness of their lack of a penis leads to strong feelings of deprivation, inferiority, and loss of love with hostility against the mother.

Because of the related pleasurable sensations during the passage of urine, and the anatomic-functional linkage of urethra and genitals, the phallic phase is intimately connected with another regularly occurring (but probably less significant) component of infantile sexuality, that of **urethral erotism.** See *oedipus complex, penis envy, preoedipal phase, psychosexual development.*

PHOBIA: Literally translated from the Greek means morbid 'fear' or 'dread'. A prefix is usually added to the word to indicate the object, condition, or circumstance dreaded. Among the more common terms are: **zoöphobia**—the fear of animals; **acrophobia**—the fear of heights; **claustrophobia**—the fear of being enclosed, especially in small places; **agoraphobia**—the fear of the street or open places. Recently there has been a trend to use a simple description of the phobia instead of the combination of Greek derivatives. The term usually connotes an unreasonable and irrational anxiety not warranted by the degree of realistic danger posed by the situation. In **phobic states** the fear is anticipated, with the development of intense *anxiety* bound to the need to avoid the circumstance feared.

Certain phobic reactions occur in the course of normal development. Fears of animals, thunder, and the dark, for example, are almost universal in childhood between two and four years of age.

In phobias the various *ego* defenses against dangerous *instinctual drives* operate in such a way that the inner danger seems to become an outer one. (See *externalization*). Unacceptable inner strivings of a sexual or aggressive nature have been repressed because of the irrational, unconscious fear of castration by the father. When these impulses threaten to emerge into *consciousness,* intense castration anxiety results in their **projection** and **displacement** onto an outside object or situation. For example, the hatred and fear of a loved father (see *ambivalence*) may be shifted finally to some animal. The advantages are evident: the elimination of conscious awareness of the hatred and fear of the father permits continued closeness to him, while the animal, to which the fear is referred, can be avoided. Though unresolved conflicts of the *oedipus complex* contribute in a major way to phobias, preoedipal problems provide a significant basis for their development.

Phobia is often used interchangeably with *anxiety hysteria* to designate the *neurosis* with which such unreasonable fears are most often associated. Phobic states, however, can be found as symptomatic manifestations in other than neurotic conditions. Phobias related to disease are frequently associated with **hypochondriasis** (excessive concern over bodily symptoms and illness) in **narcissistic neuroses,** *borderline states, depression,* and *schizophrenia.* See *anxiety hysteria.*

PLEASURE PRINCIPLE: One of what Freud called the 'regulatory principles of mental functioning'. Freud at first used the term 'unpleasure principle' and then for many years 'unpleasure-pleasure principle' before he adopted, probably for reasons of simplicity, the term 'pleasure principle'. The pleasure principle regulates the need to re-create by action, or by *fantasy,* any situation which has created the experience of satisfaction through the elimination of *drive* tension.

This principle, like the concepts *'instinctual drives'* and the *'id'*, has both biological and psychological connotations. The biological model for Freud's use of the term 'pleasure principle' was the 'constancy principle', a term coined by the father of experimental psychology, Fechner. This constancy principle, and the pleasure principle as well, assumes that the organism seeks to avoid or eliminate undue tension, which would disturb its equilibrium. Such an increase in tension is equated with unpleasure, and the elimination of tension with pleasure. The psychological concept similarly assumes that human beings strive for the achievement of gratification of various needs, equated with pleasure, as well as for the elimination of excessive tension, which is usually accompanied by unpleasure. Intolerable tension can arise either because of lack of satisfaction of wishes, or because of external and internal danger situations which would occur if they were satisfied.

The behavior of infants and small children is chiefly regulated by the pleasure principle. With progressive *maturation* the child learns that certain wishes clash with reality (for instance, one cannot jump out of a window without harm, or touch an electrical outlet), or fail to meet the requirements of the environment. The child therefore also learns, often through parental precept, warnings, and examples, the existence and importance of the *'reality principle'* (q.v.).

PRECONSCIOUS: All of the mental contents and processes which are more or less logically organized into thought patterns. These are memories, ideas, and images, and their verbal symbols as well as motor habits, which are for the most part capable of achieving *consciousness* by the act of focussing *attention.* These thought organizations may range from the purposive reflection characteristic of reality-oriented problem solving (in verbal forms) all the way to fantasies, daydreams, and dreamlike images. The term was originally applied by Freud to those mental contents capable of becoming conscious easily and under conditions which frequently arise. Their emergence into consciousness may be accompanied by widely varying reactions. The process may not be noticed, which is usual if the preconscious material is readily available to consciousness. Under other circumstances, however, its emergence into consciousness can be accompanied by strong emotional reactions. Preconscious content normally reaches consciousness by an increase in *cathexis* (generally *neutralized energy*), through the process of attention. Freud differentiated it from the content connected with unconscious processes which emerge into consciousness, if at all, only with difficulty after a considerable expenditure of energy.

PREGENITALITY: Before the psychological manifestations of overt and sublimated sexuality are unified by the activity of adult, genital discharge-patterns and *object relationships,* there is a sequence of libidinal organizations. Each of these exhibits characteristic patterns of sexual activity organized successively around the *erogenous zones*—mouth, anus, penis-clitoris—and the object relationships of the subsequent **oedipal phase** and the *latency* and prepuberty periods. The psychological derivatives of these activities in the pre-adult stages of development are manifestations of pregenitality.

In normal adults, persistent remnants of pregenitality often appear in unmodified form during the sexual foreplay prior to intercourse, and in a modified form through *sublimations* and **reaction formations,** etc. in character traits.

In *neuroses* and *psychoses,* pregenital derivatives often are channels for discharge and may exert a pathogenic and disorganizing effect. (Ed. note: It should be noted that the terms, 'pregenital' or 'pregenitality' refer to the entire period from earliest infancy to the **puberty** (adult) period when *sexual drives* and development are organized under genital primacy with ejaculatory, orgastic potential. These terms are sometimes confused, or used interchangeably, with 'prephallic' which refers specifically only to the period of the **oral** and **anal phases**) See *psychosexual development.*

PREGENITAL PHASE: See *pre-oedipal phase* and *pregenitality*. A term often misused for the *prephallic phase* which encompasses the *oral* and *anal phases* of development. Also prephallic phase is sometimes considered synonymous with *pre-oedipal phase* (since the *phallic* and *oedipal phases* overlap extensively, and are often referred to as the *phallic-oedipal phase*).

PRE-OEDIPAL PHASE: The phase of childhood development that extends from birth to the formation of the *oedipus complex* (usually at 3½ to 5 years). In contrast to the triangular situation in the latter, the pre-oedipal phase is characterized primarily by the attachment to the first *love object,* the mother. The *drive* vicissitudes involved are those of the **oral, anal** and **phallic** zones.

Some authors consider the *phallic phase* to overlap extensively with the *oedipal,* and therefore refer to the *phallic-oedipal phase.* The polarity, *active-passive,* dominates the pre-oedipal phase. In normal development, at first there is an increasing *identification* with the mother; later vicissitudes depend on variations in sexual identification. The discovery of the sex difference becomes meaningful because of phallic *masturbation* toward the end of this period. The discerning and increasing conviction that the mother is castrated then ushers in the *oedipus complex.* See *infantile sexuality, pregenitality and psychosexual development.*

PRIMAL CAVITY: The oral cavity, inclusive of cheeks, lips, the interior of the mouth, the oral and nasal pharynx. It has been observed by René Spitz, who introduced the term, that the primal cavity in the newborn is the specific body zone where perceptions of the outside and the inside of the body meet and fuse. In this primal (oral) cavity, multiple contact-type modalities of sensation are simultaneously available, such as smell and taste, touch, pain and temperature, and deep muscle sensations accompanying the swallowing reflex. With its perceptual endowment, the primal cavity is the first conglomerate sensing organ employed by the newborn for exploration of the environment. Its use for this purpose antedates the maturation of the visual mode of distance sense perception.

Participating, along with the primal cavity, in the infant's perceptions of the nursing experience are the hand, the acoustic labyrinth (both vestibular and auditory subdivisions), and the outer skin surface. See *orality*.

PRIMAL SCENE: A universal childhood recollection or *fantasy* of a couple, usually father and mother, engaging in sexual intercourse. Whether the developing child has actually observed, or only imagined this scene, it is the focus of his subsequent curiosity regarding the physical nature of the intimate relationship between his parents. As most of the world's families probably inhabit one-room dwellings, the actual childhood observation of the primal scene cannot be a rare experience, and is reflected in universal myths and customs.

For subjects who come into psychoanalytic treatment, the course of therapy at some point regularly focuses attention upon the primal scene, and especially its potentially traumatic impact upon subsequent development and emotional health. The sequelae may become manifest at any age, reflective notably of the mistaken notion of a sado-masochistic, damaging, even castrating, event. Clinically, disturbances ranging from night terrors and behavior disorder in childhood to tics, impotence, frigidity, perversion, and certain hysterical, obsessional, and manic symptoms may have reference, not necessarily causal, to the primal scene experience. Conversely, under less traumatic circumstances, primal scene fantasies may contribute to such attitudes as normal sex curiosity and appropriate sexual identification. See also *phallic phase*.

PRIMARY PROCESS: Refers both to a mode of *psychic energy* discharge and a type of thought process. The former relates to an economic concept (see *metapsychology*), with the emphasis being placed on the mobility of *cathexis* (the immediate discharge of free energy and its ready shifts in attachment) as contrasted to the bound energy with its delayed discharge that characterizes the *secondary process* (q.v.).

The second use of the term applies to a primitive, irrational type of wishful thought, dominated by the emotions and close to the *instinctual drives;* it is characterized by such features as condensation, displacement, and the extensive use of symbols. The primary process strives to achieve perceptual identity, whereas the secondary process seeks conceptual similarities. Originally conceived of as typical of the system *unconscious* and later of the *id,* it is now believed that primary process thought occurs in certain *ego* processes. Therefore, modern approaches emphasize a continuum between primary and secondary processes.

Descriptively, the term has also been applied to *affects* and action. Strong, primitive, uncontrolled emotional feelings have been designated as primary process affects in contrast to those originating in and controlled by the ego, i.e., 'tamed' or signal affects.

PSYCHIC APPARATUS (synonymous with mental apparatus): The hypothetical division of the mind on a dynamic and functional basis into various systems, agencies, or groups of functions as a conceptual aid in understanding the psychological development and behavior of human beings. It should be differentiated from the brain and its physiological activities, and no specific localization in the brain or nervous system is intended.

The more recent view of the psychic apparatus, based on the *structural theory,* divides the apparatus into systems on the basis of the criterion: inner world (manifestations of the *instinctual drives* and the *ego,* both derived from the undifferentiated ego-id matrix) versus the outer world (external environment). The earlier psychoanalytic theory, known as the *topographic hypothesis,* divided the apparatus into systems on the basis of accessibility to consciousness: systems *conscious* and *preconscious* versus the inaccessible system *unconscious.*

The growing understanding of mental functioning, and a certain incompleteness in the topographic theory, led to the formulation of the *structural theory,* which divides the mind into several groupings of psychic functions. The major division of the psychic apparatus is into two parts: 1) the *id,* which is directly related to the instinctual drives and 2) the *ego,* a more coherent and organized agency which regulates or opposes the drives, mediating between them and the demands of the external world. This division corresponds to our observations of mental function in situations of conflict. There is, however, a further division within the ego, called the *superego,* which separates off from the rest of the ego the moral and punitive functions and the ideal aspirations.

Thus, the psychic apparatus is divided into three groups of functions—*id, ego,* and *superego*—which are often referred to as psychic 'structures' (see *metapsychology*). Each of these psychic structures is more accurately understood as a group of mental contents (memory traces, memories, affective constellations, basic emotionally charged fantasies, organized thoughts, psycho-physiological associations, etc.) and processes which are functionally related to one another.

It must be emphasized that all mental activity (*fantasy,* thought, action or symptom) is the outcome of a mutual interaction among the tendencies of the id, ego and superego, combined with the influence of the external world. Psychic apparatus is the term used to refer to this total, more or less integrated, functional interaction which contributes to the final outcome of the human being's adaptation to the world.

Historically, Freud's original conception of the psychic apparatus compared it to 'different and successive systems of lenses of a telescope' in which preliminary images are formed where no tangible portion of the apparatus is located.

PSYCHIC DETERMINISM: The doctrine that all present events are influenced and largely shaped by the past, and specifically that under favorable conditions the determining factors for current human behavior, symptomatology, etc. can be understood in psychological terms. In other words, all psychic events and processes follow certain strict laws (though we may not understand these fully) and form a lawful universe similar to that of the universe of physical events and processes.

PSYCHOANALYSIS: A branch of science developed by Sigmund Freud and his followers, devoted to the study of human psychological functioning and behavior. It is usually considered to have three applications, referring to: 1) a method of investigation of the mind; 2) a systematized body of knowledge about human behavior; and 3) a method of treatment of psychological or emotional illness.

1) The method of investigation, described under *analytic process* and *analytic situation,* involves the use of *free association* and the analysis of *dreams, fantasies,* thought processes, and behavior in relation to *affects.*

2) As a branch of science devoted to the study of human psychic functions and behavior, it is a body of facts organized according to a gradually evolved system of theories (see *metapsychology, libido theory, structural theory*), applicable to normal mental development and functioning as well as to abnormal mental processes and clinical syndromes.

3) As a therapeutic method, its greatest usefulness is for the neuroses, although its principles are widely applied to other mental conditions. Briefly described, psychoanalytic treatment encourages a transient *regression* in which derivatives of forbidden wishes and repressed memories find expression in current ideas and feelings. These relate to the analyst, a relatively anonymous person to whom feelings toward important persons in the past are transferred. (See *transference*) This process enables the analyst to recognize the feelings that are residuals of past events and to reconstruct earlier traumatic situations and the conflicts associated with them. By *interpretation* these are brought into *consciousness* and their effect modified by integration of the past with the present. Through the elimination of defenses and *resistances*—based on conflict—to *perception* and memory, which determine the *unconscious* quality of some manifestations, there is an enrichment of the total personality. *Psychic energies* involved in conflict become freed and neutralized and therefore available for the synthetic and integrating functions of the *ego.* The imposed necessity for relinquishment of action during analysis facilitates the transfer of energies from the motor aspects of behavior to the psychic, thus improving the capacity to institute delay, postpone gratification, and tolerate frustration in accordance with the demands of *reality.* These are essential adaptive elements for an appropriate balance and distribution of work and recreation, and the capacity to love and be loved.

PSYCHODYNAMICS: A body of knowledge and theory of human behavior which attempts to explain the mental phenomena in normal and pathological conditions as a resultant of interacting and opposing goal-directed or motivational forces. As such, it focuses on the movement of these forces, illuminating processes, developments, progressions, and regressions. For an understanding of psychodynamics, psychoanalysis currently makes use of a *'structural'* model of the *psychic apparatus,* employing the concept of the *id* to represent the *instinctual drives,* the *ego* to represent the executive and inhibiting agencies, and the *superego* to represent the influence of conscience and idealizations; all are manifested in any psychic phenomenon. The id tensions force the organism to seek satisfaction, i.e., the discharge of tension. The drive restraining forces of the ego operate to frustrate, delay, or detour such discharge, either totally or until appropriate and safe conditions are available in *reality.* This opposition gives rise to *intrapsychic conflict;* and the results of unconscious mental arbitration may emerge into conscious awareness as a neurotic symptom. Psychodynamic considerations emphasize the importance of *unconscious* determinants of thoughts, feelings, and behavior. Innate and environmental factors are believed to be operative at all levels and in all mental structures. Genetic and developmental contributions to a present mental action would of necessity be encompassed, including *fixation* or *regression* to earlier *libidinal* or ego stages of development. These determine the nature of conflict in regard to an instinctual demand related to a specific phase. For example, an orally deprived individual may have an impairment in the *ego function* of speech in the form of stuttering, which gratifies libidinal and aggressive drives, but is experienced masochistically because the superego demands punishment for such gratification. See *metapsychology; structural theory.*

PSYCHONEUROSIS: A major category in psychoanalytic and psychiatric nomenclature designating disturbances in thought, feelings, attitudes, and behavior which have their primary origin within the mind and are only secondarily related to events and stimuli of the current real world. The term applies to a number of psychopathological entities which involve special symptom complexes. These may be involuntary movements, changes of bodily function, or odd sensations, as in *hysteria;* strong and seemingly inappropriate emotions or moods, as in anxiety attacks or *depressions;* or uncontrollable and repetitive thoughts and actions, as in *obsessions* and *compulsions.* Irrational fears, or *phobias,* characterize *anxiety hysteria.* These symptomatic manifestations are experienced by the patient as strange and unintelligible, outside the realm of the conscious will, and disturbing to usual patterns of adaptive functioning. In contrast to the phenomena of *character disorders* and *psychoses,* those of the psychoneuroses are more frequently recognized by the patient as abnormal, unwelcome, and alien to himself. In psychoneuroses, reality relationships are maintained that are lost in *psychoses,* while drive inhibitions are maintained that are lost in *perversions* and *impulse disorders.*

Psychoneuroses are the result of conflict between sexual and aggressive *drives* (*id*) and *ego* forces striving to control and limit the expression of these drives. This struggle is not based upon a realistic appraisal of the current situation, nor upon the reasonable restraint imposed by the normal *superego.* Rather, the current dangers of instinctual expression upon which the inhibiting tendency is based have their origins in *fantasies* and memory traces relating to infantile experiences when danger situations typical for successive phases of *psychosexual development* existed. (See *anxiety*) The ego reacts to the possible emergence into consciousness of these instinctual derivatives with anxiety, a danger signal which alerts and stimulates **repression** and other defensive mechanisms. Because of the continuing energy attached to the instinctual wishes, the defense against them becomes inadequate and there is a **return of the repressed** in the form of symptoms. Analysis of symptoms shows them to be **compromise formations,** disguised substitute expressions of the instinctual drives combined with manifestations of the repressing forces or even punishment by the superego. That the symptom represents the ego's efforts to integrate opposing claims of the id, superego, and *reality* is an illustration of the **principle of multiple function** described by Waelder.

Psychoneurosis is based upon *fixation* or *regression* to some phase of infantile development. Originally Freud stressed the frustration of libidinal impulses connected with the stages of *infantile sexuality,* but it is now recognized that vulnerability to psychoneurosis is dependent also on biologicaly determined factors and vicissitudes of the aggressive drives as well as the stages of maturation of the ego at which traumatic situations gave rise to conflict over the gratification of instinctual drives. A psychoneurotic illness may be precipitated when the individual finds himself in a realistic situation which corresponds to some aspect of an earlier traumatic experience. The new experience constitutes a fresh repetition of the original conflict, evoking unconscious fantasies which are a regressive reactivation of the instinctual wishes from childhood. These become the focus of renewed conflict and *symptom formation.*

Whatever distinctions once existed between the terms neuroses and psychoneuroses have been lost, and the terms are now used interchangeably. Hysteria, phobias, and the obsessive-compulsive neuroses were grouped together by Freud as *transference neuroses* because of the ready tendency of patients with those conditions to repeat the childhood neurotic pattern within the *transference* during psychoanalytic treatment. Because of their lesser capacity for object relationships, patients with *melancholia* and schizophrenia did not show this tendency to the same degree and these entities were therefore termed **narcissistic neuroses.** See *'actual neurosis'*, *anxiety*, *intrapsychic conflict*, *neurosis*, and *symptom formation.*

PSYCHOSEXUAL DEVELOPMENT: The concept of psychosexual development resulted from Freud's painstaking examination of the origin and dynamics of neurotic symptoms. He recognized a regular sequence of libidinal manifestations beginning in early infancy and continuing to adulthood. The early phases, described under *infantile sexuality,* are centered on and organized around the oral, anal, and later the phallic zones. These libidinal manifestations consist of pleasure giving activities, predominantly sucking (and later biting) at the oral phase, expulsion and retention of feces during the anal phase, and finally manipulation (infantile *masturbation*) of the phallus (penis or clitoris) in the *phallic phase.* Each of these bodily activities is accompanied by more or less typical mental phenomena, connected mainly with objects of the child's surrounding world. Reference to these specific psychosexual stages therefore connotes more than the physical activity associated with it; also included are the psychic gratifications and frustrations, derivative mental and behavioral phenomena, and the accompanying conflicts. The phallic phase, for example, highlights the significant differences between the sexes. It is typified by special interest in the naked body, curiosity about the opposite sex, and a wish to look at (**scopophilia**) and to have the genitals seen (**exhibitionism**). In the female child, it is often marked by a sense of inadequacy about her genital organs, *penis envy,* and competitive, masculine strivings. The conflicts arising from this period are predominately related to the *oedipus complex,* the resolution of which determines the choice of an object for genital satisfaction, and the final sexual orientation and *identification* of the individual.

Childhood psychosexual development undergoes a typical arrest with the development of the *castration complex* in connection with oedipal fantasies. Beginning at about age six, a period of relative quiescence of sexual activity, called *latency,* ensues. With the onset of puberty, psychosexual development is resumed, culminating, if successful, in the *genital phase.* Normally, after this stage is reached, the pleasures characteristic of the earlier infantile period are manifested in the sexual act only in so-called forepleasure. If the infantile pleasures remain the sole aim of sexual strivings in adults, the activities are called *perversions.* Psychic derivatives of the earlier libidinal stages are, however, often residual components in character structure and symptoms, or more constructively, they may contribute to professional and artistic achievement.

Manifestations of the aggressive drive appear with the development of teeth and motor coordination, but its psychological association is probably most strikingly correlated with the anal phase. In general, development of the aggressive drive proceeds concomitantly with psychosexual development, the same zones being involved, but stages in aggressive development have not been so definitively described. See *anality, character formation, infantile sexuality, instinctual drives, libido theory, orality, phallic phase, symptom formation.*

PSYCHOSIS: A form of mental disorder associated with severe personality disorganization and characterized by marked *ego* and *libidinal regression.* There are two general groupings of psychoses, the organic and the functional. The former are secondary to physical disease (e.g. syphilitic general paresis, brain tumor, arteriosclerosis, etc.) while the latter are related to constitutional, biological and psychological factors. The major functional psychoses are 1) the affective disorders—manic-depressive psychosis and 2) the thought disorders—schizophrenia and true paranoia. There have been many controversies about the psychoses (esp. schizophrenia) concerning the relative importance of the hereditary, constitutional, neuro-endocrine, various somatic and metabolic patterns, and psychological-environmental factors. Whatever may be eventually discovered about each of the above factors, it seems certain that individual psychological reactions and experiences will have a major and most significant role in the etiology (cause) of both process and *symptom formation.*

The phenomenological characteristics of the psychoses are, to a greater or lesser degree, bizarre behavior, delusional ideas, inappropriately labile and intense *affective* reactions, withdrawal, and a significant disturbance in contact with reality and the sense of *reality*. Hallucinatory experiences, difficulty in communication (esp. loose associations and thought connections) and hypochondriasis are often prominent features.

Freud originally conceptualized the psychopathology of the psychoses in such a way as to emphasize a fundamental unity between the mental processes in psychoses and neuroses. However, he also pointed out certain significant differences; the psychotic individual is unconsciously fixated to an earlier level of libidinal development, the *narcissistic* phase. This leads to the most important feature in the development of psychosis—the change in the patient's relationship with the persons and objects of the world about him. Thus, other individuals are seen to be both withdrawn and detached, often with a strongly hostile attitude; this is usually related to the idea that the world and the people in it have somehow changed, which sometimes extends into a 'world destruction' fantasy ('the world is destroyed' or 'everything and everybody is unreal'). Freud regarded this group of symptoms as representing the patient's break with reality—the most characteristic single feature of the psychoses.

The above may be considered the first stage of a two-stage process. In the first stage (the narcissistic regression), the mental representations of external persons and objects are decathected, and the *libido* freed to cathect the patient's *self*. In the second or restitutive stage, there is an attempt to recathect those *object representations,* leading to an attempt to re-establish contact, often pathological, with the outer world (manifested frequently by delusions and hallucinations). Occasionally, if restitution is more successful, it leads to a partial recovery.

Recently various analytic observers have suggested, with considerable clinical and theoretical evidence, that the later concepts of Freud's *structural theory,* particularly the concept of *regression* of *ego functions,* explain the clinical phenomena of the psychosis better than do his earlier concepts of libidinal decathexis and recathexis. They suggest the great majority of the alterations in the *ego* and *superego* functions which characterize the psychosis are part of the *defense* against the emergence of *anxiety*. These defensive alterations in ego functions are so extensive as to disrupt the patient's *object relationships* to such a degree that it can be considered a break with reality.

In simpler terms, psychoses have been differentiated from the *neuroses* by Freud on the basis of certain characteristic differences. In neurosis, there is, first, the *repression* of the prohibited demand of the *id* and, second, its return in a distorted form (*symptom formation*). In the development of psychosis, there is the decathexis of object representations (the break with reality) and, secondly, the attempts to regain the lost reality. In neurosis, it is the return of the repressed which has the major impact, while in psychosis, it is the loss of reality. In neurosis, the struggle is predominantly between the *instinctual drives* of the id and the defensive processes of the ego; while in the psychosis, it is the id (and in part, the superego) which, having overwhelmed the ego defenses, comes into conflict with a frustrating reality, which then can only be dealt with by its fantasied destruction and distorted restitution.

The investigation of the psychoses led Freud and other observers into a re-evaluation of the earlier *libido* and *topographic theories*. A better understanding of *narcissism,* the *aggressive drive,* and the concept of the *self* contributed to the development of the structural theory and the dual instinct theory, resulting finally in the more significant place of ego psychology in psychoanalysis. It has also encouraged and facilitated the study of early ego states and development because of their significance in psychotic regression.

Generally, psychoanalytic therapy has been focussed on the *neuroses,* and later the *character neuroses* and *perversions*. Recently, as part of the 'widening scope of psychoanalysis', psychoanalytic technique has been applied to selected cases of psychoses. Various degrees of success have been reported; usually, however, certain *parameters* from the classical method are necessary.

Originally it was felt that 'no transference' relationship could develop in such cases because of the degree of narcissism; however a more accurate description is that quite intense and distorted *transferences* (sometimes described as transference psychosis) develop which have to be handled and resolved with great care since they often represent the patient's initial and very tenuous efforts to re-establish a genuine *object relationship* with another human being. See *borderline states, character disorders, paranoid, psychoneurosis, psychotic character, regression.*

PSYCHOTIC CHARACTER: A personality disturbance which is viewed as a specific and recognizable clinical entity, the counterpart of the neurotic character. It is roughly synonymous with *borderline personality*. As in the neurotic character, elements of *intrapsychic conflict* are crystallized into the character structure in such a way as to bring about predictable modes of *adaptation* and response to stress. Though the individual is not psychotic, these modes of responding are frequently governed by the same features underlying psychotic reactions. Under stress, therefore, it is to be expected that anxieties, reactive patterns, and impairment of functions similar to those of the psychotic will develop. Indeed, psychotic symptoms do become manifest in some individuals, but they are reversible in contrast to those of the psychotic, and it is possible for many identifiable psychotic characters to go through life without showing psychotic symptomatology.

A proclivity for marked *regression* and loss of differentiation of *self* and non-self (all the external world, including objects) is usually accompanied by the capacity to reverse these processes. *Object relations* are established, but on a more infantile level than those of 'normal' and neurotic individuals. Although severely impaired, the relationship to *reality*, the sense of reality, and the ability to test reality is, in contrast to the psychotic, generally preserved.

The term should not be used for a transitional phase on the way to or from *psychosis*, but should be reserved for individuals who have such identifiable features as an integral part of their character structure. See *borderline personality, character disorders, character formation, ego functions*, and *psychosis*.

REALITY: A concept which is understood and used in a number of different ways and contexts. One may distinguish between reality as it appears to an objective, adult observer, brought up in a scientific tradition, and reality as it is experienced in evolving stages of development in the emotional and intellectual life of the individual.

Psychic reality designates the totality of a person's mental representation of his physical-instinctual life and of his thoughts, feelings, *dreams* and *fantasies*, memories, and *perceptions*—regardless of whether or not they accurately reflect or correspond to objective reality. This totality comprises both *conscious* and *unconscious* elements; the latter may be apprehended and understood, or inferred by the specific method of *psychoanalysis*. Particular attention is paid by the analyst to unconscious processes and contents, which are often considered to be the true psychic reality underlying their more superficial, conscious manifestations.

The development of the **sense of objective reality** (including the capacity for assessing its elements, i.e., **reality-testing**) is a gradually unfolding process of distinguishing between inside and outside (subject and *object*); differentiating between past, present, and future; and moving from *narcissistic* and magical ways of experiencing reality to a more rational view. The basic outlines of this transformation of reality are established during the first five or six years of life, and are closely interwoven with the development of language and the establishment of firm *object relations* during the *oedipal period.* Older, less rational forms of organizing reality persist, however, throughout life to a greater or lesser degree, side by side with later ones.

Much of what the child perceives and experiences in his relations with external reality is assimilated into his *ego,* and structures his psychic reality. In this sense, both ego and *superego* are considered to be derived from the interaction between the primitive psyche and reality. Inner psychic reality thus is shaped by external reality, and shapes external reality as well, through action and word expressing this inner life.

In *psychotic* and *borderline states* we often find a withdrawal from reality or *regression* to primitive, infantile ways of organizing reality. In *neurosis,* especially in the character neurosis, such regression takes place too, but not to the same degree, and the patient's rational-intellectual processes remain relatively unaffected.

External reality: The outer world of the individual's environment, as distinguished from the reality of his psychic life. From the observer's point of view, external reality is the objective world of persons and things, of time-space and causal relationships; however, associated with the development of the *ego,* this objective external reality only gradually becomes organized as stages in the development of the sense of reality. This development begins with discriminations between inside and outside (the setting up of **ego boundaries**) and of past, present and future—distinctions which are not present at first. A young child, for instance, still finds it difficult to distinguish between his *fantasies* and actual occurrences in the external world, and between his own feelings and those of his mother. At a still earlier stage, he is even unable to distinguish between his own body and the parts of his mother's body which are emotionally significant to him. The boundaries between ego and external reality are at first non-existent, and remain uncertain and blurred during early childhood. The development of **object-constancy** (the ability to maintain an internal representation of the loved object even in its physical absence) is an important element in the constitution of external reality. The emotional experiences of the **oedipal period** are also necessary ingredients of this whole process.

Disturbances of the discrimination between ego and external reality are seen in many pathological conditions, especially in *psychosis,* but also in certain drug-induced states; they may, however, occur normally during periods of going to sleep or waking up. Hallucinations and dreams are special states of altered *consciousness* in which there is a lack or suspension of such discrimination.

REALITY PRINCIPLE: The uninhibited and unmodified search for the satisfaction of needs and wishes and the avoidance of pain is gradually replaced, in the course of normal development, by modes of action and thought which take into account, and are shaped by the exigencies and conditions of real life. Logic and the rational appraisal of cause-effect relations in the outside world, as well as a growing awareness and understanding of oneself and of the needs, feelings, demands, actions and thoughts of other people, increasingly determine behavior and tame the *instinctual drives.* This process is conceptualized as the substitution of the reality principle for the *pleasure principle.* When a child postpones going out to play in order to do his homework first, when a man or woman foregoes the pleasures of a sexual affair in the interest of good marital relations, their behavior is governed by the reality principle. The change from being ruled by the *pleasure principle* to the more restrained and rational forms of thought, feelings, and action characteristic of the reality principle, involves delays, postponements, renunciations and other more complex inhibitions and transformations of drive discharge and need satisfaction. The *ego,* being structured by the psyche's relations with (external) *reality,* is more under the sway of the reality principle, whereas the *id* remains and operates under the sway of the pleasure principle. See *pleasure principle, reality.*

RECONSTRUCTION: An important type of *intervention* used in the course of psychoanalytic treatment. It consists of the analyst's attempt—one of his chief tasks—to correlate, understand, and then convey to his patient (i.e., to reconstruct) forgotten, repressed, but psychologically important early experiences from the traces that they have left behind. Such traces gradually emerge in the patient's *free associations,* behavior, *dreams,* and *transference* reactions. The latter provide especially significant data for this form of intervention. Reconstruction is a gradual process, slowly and carefully advanced, which often leads to the further recall by the patient of repressed memories or other associations supplying new data for deeper understanding and interpretation. Reconstruction has been compared to the work of the archaeologist, who extrapolates a description of aspects of past civilizations from fragments and traces found in the present. *Psychoanalysis,* however, is now a more complex process than it was originally, when the recovery of the repressed memories of childhood traumatic experiences was the single most important occurrence in treatment. This is no longer true.

Nevertheless, reconstructions are still an essential part of psychoanalytic therapy because repressed early experiences are highly charged with emotional conflict. They have a serious impact on development and personality formation, and play a major role in the origin and perpetuation of psychopathology. Thus the importance of reconstruction derives from the significance of the genetic (i.e., developmental) nature of psychoanalytic psychology, which stresses the historical roots of behavior. The latter are often uncovered and understood by means of reconstruction. See *character formation, development, interpretation, metapsychology, symptom formation.*

REGRESSION: A concept which can best be described under two headings:

A. **Libidinal Regression:** A retreat to an earlier phase of instinctual organization, especially of the infantile period. Such a falling back occurs if, in the life process, a biologically predetermined *maturational* step presents the individual with difficulties which he is unable to master. Often this is determined by unresolved conflicts and anxieties at earlier phases which leave 'areas of weakness' in the preceding developmental phases (i.e. *fixations*) to which the individual is more likely to regress. A simple example of regression may be observed when, at times of emotional stress, a five year old child resumes thumb-sucking, a habit he had previously abandoned, or after engaging in genital masturbatory play, returns to anal *masturbation*. In childhood, when the development of sexual *drives* is still fluid, such regressions are ubiquitous (e.g. at times of illness or fatigue), and do not necessarily indicate pathology. Normal adults also show recurrence of archaic patterns of instinctual wishes and behavior under certain conditions, such as states of sleep and *dreaming*, or while under the influence of drugs and intoxicants. Pathological manifestations of regression are found in the symptoms of *neuroses* and *psychoses*, as well as in the *perversions*.

If heterosexual genital sexuality confronts an individual with *anxiety* and guilt feelings which cannot be mastered, he may fall back to some form of *infantile sexuality*, replacing genital sexuality with some prephallic form, and thus develop a perversion. In this instance, the regression serves as a *defense*, protecting the individual against the intolerable anxiety which genital sexuality arouses in him.

B. **Ego Regression:** From a more highly developed stage of mental organization, the mind may revert to modes of functioning typical of an earlier period. This 'regression' usually affects only certain ego functions involved in conflict, but the form of representations and the formal quality of ideas are usually affected. Such reacquisition of old patterns is a frequent accompaniment of libidinal regression, and occurs in response to a variety of needs that arise from internal and external pressures.

The causes of regression are manifold, e.g. unpleasurable feelings (anxiety, guilt); mental pathology (neurotic and psychotic processes); bodily pathology (especially when the central nervous system is affected); disorganization of functioning caused by drugs; and so forth. The most common cause of regression in the neuroses probably is the unresolved *oedipus complex* with its associated *castration anxiety, penis envy,* and guilt-evoking unconscious sexual and aggressive impulses.

The concept of regression is intimately related to the hypothesis that, in the course of attaining adulthood, an individual passes through a series of maturational phases (*psychosexual development*), each with a phase-appropriate mental organization. The make-up of each such organization is inferred from the way a) instinctual drives discharge; b) ego functions operate; and c) conscience and ideals guide. When a phase-appropriate organization is substantially disrupted, regression occurs.

REPETITION COMPULSION: Clinically, this phenomenon represents a general tendency in all human behavior to repeat painful experiences. In the course of living out their lives, some individuals go through a recurring series of unsettling, stressful episodes or phases which, because they develop quite unexpectedly and are apparently unrelated to the individual's personality or general behavior, tend to be attributed to the operation of 'bad luck' or 'destiny'. Persons with such recurrent life tragedies, each usually similar to the others in terms of the configuration of the stress imposed and the adaptive response evoked, are sometimes said to be suffering from 'fate neurosis' or from the operation of the 'repetition compulsion'. Among its other varied manifestations are the repetitions in children's play that serve to master the experience of loss, recurrent nightmares after a traumatic event, the re-enactment of childhood conflicts during *psychoanalytic treatment* (see *acting out*), and certain *character disorders* with a persistent need for self-defeating behavior.

This clinical syndrome, so interesting in its dramatic and enigmatic phenomenology, is important for an understanding of how the mind is progressively structured during development and its functioning regulated by basic psychological principles. An illustration of this is the finding that the operation of the repetition compulsion, in contrast to the operation of all other investigated psychological phenomena including *masochism,* seems to be relatively uninfluenced or unregulated by the *pleasure-unpleasure principle.* This characteristic struck Sigmund Freud so forcibly that he gave his first published study of the repetition compulsion the title, *Beyond the Pleasure Principle;* and he used this characteristic as a means of differentiating mental operations that are more primitive in a biological-evolutionary sense from those operations that are regulated by the pleasure-unpleasure principle.

The repetition compulsion was also used by Freud to develop his theory of the life and death instincts. Other psychoanalytic workers have dealt with the syndrome in various other ways: relating it to the *ego's function* of mastery, redefining it as a variant of masochism, or identifying it as one manifestation of those biological *drives* that are responsible for the *maturation* of mental structure and functioning (drives that press for discharge despite the operation of the pleasure-unpleasure principle). See *instinct, pleasure principle.*

RESISTANCE: A technical term referring to a phenomenon encountered in the course of psychoanalytic treatment. The psychic equilibrium of a person rests on the balance of inner psychic forces, and the disturbance of this equilibrium causes *anxiety.* People tend, therefore, to oppose automatically anything that disturbs the inner balance, regardless of the fact that they may know that the interference with the established balance might be to their long term advantage (somewhat in the way that people are ready to oppose the probing of the dentist, even before the probing hurts). In the simplest case, the inner balance consists of a wish or urge that is held in check by a counterforce (an internal prohibition). During the psychoanalytic treatment the patient is encouraged to talk about the activities going on in his mind. As he does so (see *free association*), he becomes increasingly aware of the prohibitive-defense part of his mind as well as of the wishes and urges which are held in check by the prohibitions. The mere awareness, however, endangers the inner balance; the patient unconsciously blames the analyst and the analytic method for disturbing this balance and for causing him anxiety; and he begins to oppose the analysis and the analyst. This opposition (which takes a variety of forms) is called resistance.

SECONDARY PROCESS: Predominantly logical, controlled thinking characterized economically by the use of minimal amounts of *neutralized psychic energy* as opposed to the free *fantasies* and massive discharges of unbound energy involved in the *primary process*. There are considered to be many thought forms transitional between primary and secondary process, as in creative mental activities, daydreaming, and in psychopathological conditions such as paranoia and *obsessions*. Even in *dreams*, conceived largely as a *primary process* manifestation of the *id*, defensive and controlling activities of the *ego* in the form of the secondary process can be observed.

Secondary process also characteristically introduces the concept of delay, or postponement, of immediate discharge—obviously a necessary condition for logical thought—as contrasted with primary process which strives for immediate discharge. See *ego, primary process*.

SELF: The total person of an individual in *reality*, including his body and psychic organization; one's 'own person' as contrasted with 'other persons' and objects outside one's self. The 'self' is a common-sense concept; its clinical and *metapsychological* aspects are treated under *self image, self representation*, etc. See *ego, identity, narcissism*.

SELF IMAGE: The image which an individual has of himself at a particular time in a specific situation. It consists of his *body image* and the representation of his inner state at the time. The *ego* constructs the self image from the direct experiences of sensations, emotions, and thoughts, and from indirect perceptions of the bodily and mental self as an object. A self image may be conscious or unconscious, realistic or unrealistic. A conscious self image may mirror realistically all the physical, emotional, and mental features of an individual, or it may be unrealistic because of distortions resulting from the repression of unacceptable features and their substitution by fantasied ones in accordance with the individual's wishes and defensive needs. In the latter case, the realistic self image is unconscious. See *self representation*.

SELF REPRESENTATION: A more enduring schema than the *self image* (q.v.), constructed by the *ego* out of the multitude of realistic and distorted self images which the individual has had at different times. It represents the person as he consciously and unconsciously perceives himself. It includes enduring representations of all the experienced body states, and all the experienced *drives* and *affects* which the individual has consciously or unconsciously perceived in himself at different times in reaction to himself and to the outer world. Together with the object representations, it provides the material for all the ego's adaptive and defensive functions. See *self image*.

SEPARATION ANXIETY: A descriptive term, which refers to the painful *affect* of *anxiety* engendered by the threat of, or actual physical separation from a loved one. This is a normal reaction, if not excessive, in the first years of life, during which time the child is largely dependent on the mother for his survival and care and has not yet overcome his fear of losing her. In later childhood or adulthood, if excessive and inappropriate to the situation, separation anxiety represents a multi-determined symptom with a number of underlying meanings. One of these, excessive *ambivalence* toward the loved person, is invariably present and often the most significant. The absence of the loved person creates the possibility that unconscious hostile wishes may become fulfilled, and unrealistic anxiety ensues. The presence of the ambivalently loved person serves as a reassurance against death wishes, since it is apparent that no harm has occurred. See *anxiety, object loss, depression.*

SOMATIZATION: The tendency to react to stimuli (including *instinctual drives,* defenses, and the ensuing *conflict*) with physical (i.e., somatic, bodily) rather than psychic manifestations. The infant reacts to painful stimulation with a host of somatic responses. With progressive *maturation,* however, somatic responses to stimuli are replaced by action and/or thought processes. This development has been called 'de-somatization' of responses. Some individuals, suffering from conflict not resolved by neurotic mechanisms, regress to the earlier somatic type of response. This 're-somatization' of responses plays a major role in 'psychosomatic disorders.' Actual physiological, and often pathological, changes take place in the organs or body systems so affected, although the psycho-physiological mechanisms by which the mind affects the body have not been fully clarified. Examples of re-somatization are the psychosomatic conditions of ulcerative colitis, asthma, essential hypertension, and various skin disorders.

SPLITTING OF THE EGO: Although the normal *ego* is essentially a relatively unified and organized group of functions, there are circumstances under which particular functions of the ego are set up against others, at least temporarily. For example, this occurs in the act of self observation. One thinks, feels, and acts subjectively, but at the same time observes such behavior in a quasi-objective manner. In the psychoanalytic situation such a splitting of the ego is a regular and necessary occurrence. The interpretative action of the analyst helps the patient to become aware of and observe his own drive-directed or defensive experiences, mostly in the transference, and to recognize them as a repetition of past attitudes and experiences (often repressed). Thus the ego is 'split' into sets of functions which can best be described as the observing aspect and the experiencing aspect. In this way, in therapeutic cooperation with the analyst, the patient can view his own activities and reactions while he is at the same time experiencing them, often with their full affective charge. This 'therapeutic split' of the ego is temporary and is replaced by integration of the previously unconscious material into the ego. More permanent ego dissociations are the cause of serious psychopathology (e.g. dual personality, fugue states, many forms of *perversion,* and *psychosis,* etc.).

One classic example is that afforded by the fetishist. He is consciously aware of the anatomy of the female genitals and behaves in accordance with that knowledge; but by requiring a fetish, a symbolic substitute for the female phallus, as a necessary prerequisite for his potency in sexual intercourse, he acts out an unconscious fantasy denying the difference between the sexes.

STRUCTURAL THEORY: The currently accepted psychoanalytic theory of mental functioning which Freud advanced in 1923. It differs in its explanatory potential, and in other significant ways, from the earlier *topographic theory*. (See *topography, psychic apparatus*).

According to the structural theory, the mind (*psychic apparatus*) is divided into three functional groups which are called *ego, id* and *superego*. These are called 'structures' because of the relative constancy of their objectives and consistency in modes of operation. This division corresponds to what one can observe as to how the mind functions in situations of *conflict* over an *instinctual drive*. The major division is in two parts—one part, the id, is directly related to the *instinctual drives,* while the other, the ego, is more coherent and more organized. It regulates or opposes the drives, mediating between them and the demands of the external world. The structural theory makes a second division within the ego itself, separating from the rest of the ego certain moral functions, collectively called the superego. See *ego, id, superego.*

SUBLIMATION: The deflection of the energies of *instinctual drives* to aims that are more acceptable to the *ego* and *superego*. Especially involved are those energies related to the satisfaction of oral and anal wishes (the pre-oedipal *libido*). Transformations of the energy itself, effected largely through the mechanism of *identification,* are emphasized in the related concept of *neutralization* (q.v.). The pleasures and achievements of artistic and intellectual creativity have provided traditional illustrations of sublimation, though in a larger sense all conflict-free activities that promote the synthesis of the total personality may be regarded in this category. Inadequacies or failures of sublimation, whether constitutional or developmental, may contribute to *perversions,* psychopathic behavior, and other adaptive disorders. See *conflict-free ego sphere, neutralization,* and *psychic energy.*

SUPEREGO: A theoretical concept designating those psychic functions which, in their manifest expression, represent moral attitudes, conscience, and the sense of guilt. It results from the *internalization* of the ethical standards of the society in which the person lives, and develops by *identification* with the attitudes of parents and other significant persons in the child's environment. Superego functions may be divided into two categories: 1) the protective and rewarding functions, which set up ideals and values that are grouped under the term, *ego-ideal;* 2) the critical and punishing functions which evoke the sense of guilt and the pangs of conscience. In the *structural theory,* the superego is one of the three component parts or systems of the *psychic apparatus.* In neuroses, symptoms arise as compromises in the conflict between *instinctual drives* (*id* derivatives) and the forces seeking to forbid or restrain their expression (the superego). Such conflict is described as inter-systemic. See *ego ideal, internalization, psychic apparatus, structural theory.*

SYMBIOSIS: A term introduced by Margaret Mahler in 1950 to describe the interdependent condition of the human infant and his mother, who creates a 'kind of social symbiosis' after birth, acting thereby as the child's protector or 'buffer', since he lacks an independent capacity for self-preservation. The term also refers to the stage of *object* or 'pre-object' *relationship* in which self and maternal intrapsychic representations have not yet been differentiated. In symbiotic child psychosis there is a regression to a pathological form of this early phase of development.

SYMBOLISM: A form of indirect representation first noted among primitive people, and in the symptoms and *dreams* of neurotic patients. It is like a secret language in which, for example, money is represented by feces, or windows equated with the opening of the female genitals. Early in the history of psychoanalysis, the ideas or objects so represented were found to be charged with inappropriate feelings and laden with conflict, and the meanings of the symbols were forbidden ones which remained unconscious. Symbols were at first thought to be universal and inherited; later the apparent universality was seen to be attributable to the similarity of interests and experiences among infants. It follows that the most common subjects of symbolism are body parts and functions, family members, birth, and death. Functionally, the symbol disguises the unacceptable, while allowing partial gratification or the retention of a lost object. Questions still exist with regard to how early in life the process occurs, to what extent it requires some alteration in the state of consciousness (such as in sleep or illness), and whether it must be associated with conflict. Recent interest in *ego* functioning stresses the broader aspects of symbolism. It is now believed to be the most uniquely human trait involved in all mental activity—from primitive symbol formation through literary and artistic forms, mathematics, and the most abstract forms of thinking. See *dreams, primary process.*

SYMPTOM FORMATION: Psychoneurotic symptoms derive from *unconscious* psychic *conflict* arising from contending forces within the individual. These forces consist of repressed derivatives (unconscious *fantasies, impulses,* wishes) of childhood *instinctual drives* (both sexual and aggressive)—especially closely associated with the *oedipal stage* of *development*—and those psychic structures (*ego, superego*) which oppose the entrance of such derivatives into conscious thought or behavior for moral or reality-adaptive reasons.

Such unconscious conflict is, however, universal and unavoidable; childhood instinctual conflicts may have other outcomes than symptom formation. For example, they may give rise to stable defensive patterns which play a major role in *character formation;* they may be sufficiently resolved to permit either a degree of acceptable direct gratification or a highly modified expression in useful *sublimations.*

When in the course of life, however, the equilibrium between the instinctual and the repressive forces is disturbed (either through the strengthening of the former, as in puberty, or the weakening of the latter, as in physical illness), the repressed drive derivatives threaten to emerge into *consciousness,* giving rise thereby to *anxiety* or guilt. If the latter affective responses are so intense as to go beyond their signal function (see *anxiety*), then symptoms usually develop. Such symptoms are **compromise formations** which simultaneously consist of 1) a partial, substitute gratification of drive derivatives and the unconscious fantasy wishes associated with them, and 2) the opposition of repressing and adaptive psychic agencies, which results in a highly disguised, incomplete, and therefore consciously unrecognizable form of drive expression.

A further aspect of this complex compromise is represented by the suffering associated with most neurotic symptoms. This satisfies the unconscious demand for self-punishment made necessary by the substitute gratification of conflictual drive derivatives achieved in the symptom.

Psychoneurotic symptoms thus permit the sufferer to avoid some of the guilt and anxiety that a full, undisguised breakthrough of instinctual derivatives would produce.

Particular symptoms, and the specific illnesses characterized by them, arise from the complex variations in the nature of the neurotic conflict, the differences in instinctual forces and the defenses employed, the nature and intensity of the external stresses and traumas, the strengths and weaknesses of the *psychic apparatus* and its component parts, and the character structure and life experiences of the individual who falls sick.

TOPOGRAPHY: The special branch of psychoanalytic theory that attempts to classify mental operations and contents according to 'regions' in the mental apparatus. These regions are neither anatomical nor spatial, but rather are described according to their relationship to *consciousness.* Thus, a mental event (a wish, idea, or feeling) that occurs outside of conscious awareness, and cannot be made conscious by the effort of focussing attention, is said to occur in the 'deepest' region of the mind, 'the *unconscious*'. A mental event which can be brought to conscious awareness by an act of attention is said to be *'preconscious'* which is hence not as 'deep' in the mind as the unconscious. Finally, there are mental events which occur in conscious awareness and are thus located on the 'surface' of the mind.

The topographical viewpoint implies that a mental event and its contents have been described in terms of these 'regions'. In current psychoanalytic theory, the topographic hypothesis has been largely supplanted by the *structural theory* of the *mental apparatus.* However, the topographic system is still useful in describing the quality and degree of awareness of mental events and content. See *consciousness, preconscious* and *unconscious.*

TRANSFERENCE: The *displacement* of patterns of feelings and behavior, originally experienced with significant figures of one's childhood, to individuals in one's current relationships. This *unconscious* process thus brings about a repetition, not consciously perceived, of attitudes, *fantasies* and emotions of love, hate, anger, etc. under many different circumstances. The parents are usually the original figures from whom such patterns are displaced, but in many instances siblings, grandparents, childhood teachers and doctors may be contributing figures.

The types of transference include intra- and extra-analytic, as well as positive and negative. In most analytic and psychiatric writings, the term transference, when unmodified, refers to **intra-analytic transference. Extra-analytic transference** covers a wide range of circumstances (including its occurrence in psychotherapy, other medical relationships, as well as in school, office, home and social interactions). Potentially, it may develop in any relationship between two human beings.

Intra-analytic transference is of major significance in the *analytic process.* The demonstration, *interpretation* and resolution of transference in the analytic situation constitutes the core of analytic therapy. Thus the technical procedures of *psychoanalysis* are in part designed to encourage and facilitate *regression* with the concomitant unfolding of the transference. Intra-analytic transference achieves a major impact in treatment from the fact that these feelings and attitudes are directed toward the person of the analyst, and eventually develop into the *transference neurosis.*

Positive transference refers to the analytic situation where predominantly friendly, affectionate and/or intense sexual wishes and fantasies are felt toward the analyst; **negative transference** refers to the situation where predominantly aggressive, hostile, or even sadistic wishes are experienced toward the analyst. These transference feelings are far more complex than this simple designation of attitude suggests.

One of the important reasons for the relative anonymity of the analyst during the treatment process is the fact that a lack of information about his real attributes and personal life facilitates the transfer of the patient's revived early images on to his person. It also lessens the distortion of fantasies from the past by present perceptions. It must be recognized that there are situations or circumstances where the actual behavior or attitudes of the analyst cause reactions in the patient; these are not considered part of the transference reaction. (See *counter-transference*).

Also, transference should be carefully differentiated from the **therapeutic alliance,** a conscious aspect of the relationship between analyst and patient. In this, each implicitly agrees and understands their working together to help the analysand mature through *insight,* progressive understanding and control. It involves a therapeutic split in the patient's ego, with one area of *ego functioning* cooperating with the analyst by observing the other experiencing part of the ego. A strong therapeutic alliance is often essential to the continuation of the analysis during periods of strong negative transference. See *splitting of the ego.*

TRANSFERENCE NEUROSIS: Historically, this term was used by Freud to designate those *psychoneuroses* which are most amenable to treatment by classical *psychoanalysis,* namely *hysteria, anxiety hysteria* and *obsessional neurosis.* These were contrasted especially with the *'actual' neuroses* and the *psychoses,* also called *narcissistic neuroses* by Freud.

In the modern terminology, transference neurosis is the new 'version' of the neurosis which develops in the course of psychoanalytic treatment, with the analyst as the focal figure upon whom the original childhood *conflicts* between *instinctual drives* and the *defenses* against them are now displaced. This substitution of a transference neurosis for the clinical neurosis is only rarely complete. The transference neurosis is an indispensable therapeutic tool, since the feelings experienced by the patient in the *transference* have a unique vividness in the present, which makes their *interpretation* and the sense of conviction about them especially effective. If transference is used by the patient as a resistance that proves difficult to overcome, the possibility of successful psychoanalytic treatment will be correspondingly diminished. See *analytic process, psychoanalysis, psychoneurosis, transference.*

TRANSITIONAL OBJECT: The infant's first possession, a blanket or toy which he holds and manipulates on going to sleep and in times of distress. It is often associated with finger sucking and given up when this habit disappears. A special texture and smell may identify such an object as uniquely the infant's own. A link between himself and his mother, the transitional object contains qualities of both mother and child.

The transitional object has illusory aspects, along with toys and dolls, which are endowed with animate qualities in childhood. While a normal phenomenon in childhood and in many creative experiences throughout life, a transitional object can become a point of departure for abnormal developments, as in delinquent acting out, addiction, *perversions,* and inappropriate behavior during analysis. See *object choice.*

TRAUMA: A stimulus, arising from an external situation or from massive inner sexual and aggressive excitement, which is experienced as overwhelming the ego's capacity to mediate between the various forces making demands on it. Such stimuli are usually sudden and disruptive, and produce a state of helplessness ranging from apathetic inactivity to emotional storm. Traumatic events are usually followed by marked regressive phenomena, severe inhibitions, and physical symptoms reflecting autonomic dysfunction.

TRAUMATIC NEUROSIS: A neurosis in which overwhelming tension and painful *affects,* such as *anxiety* or guilt related to a traumatic experience, can not be mastered by the usual defenses of the *ego.* Pathological and archaic ego mechanisms are set in motion which determine a clinical picture dominated by somatic features and a *repetition compulsion* forcibly bringing to mind the original trauma. Symptoms include marked emotional lability, with uncontrollable discharges of anxiety, fear, or rage; severe disturbances of sleep, with typical dreams in which the trauma is painfully reexperienced; and mental repetitions in the waking state of the traumatic situation, in whole or in part, in the form of *fantasies,* thoughts, or feelings. Psychological mastery of the trauma is usually accompanied by recession of the traumatic elements and increasing prominence of psychoneurotic symptoms.

UNCONSCIOUS: The quality of not being conscious or within mental awareness, typical of certain mental content, or of the dynamic state of such content or processes. It may be described from several different standpoints:

A. **Descriptive Unconscious:** The aggregate of all mental contents and processes which at any given moment are outside of conscious awareness (or are 'unnoticed'). This of course includes all those contents of the mind which are *'preconscious'.*

B. **Dynamic Unconscious:** Those mental contents and processes of the 'system' unconscious which are incapable of achieving *consciousness* because of the operation of a counterforce known as *repression* (or censorship). This force manifests itself during psychoanalytic treatment as a *resistance* to remembering.

Unconscious mental contents consist of *drive* representations and wishes, which are unacceptable, threatening or abhorrent to the moral, ethical and intellectual standards of the individual. They nevertheless strive continuously for discharge in behavior or thought; this striving results in *intrapsychic conflict* and may produce feelings of *anxiety* or guilt. Should the counterforce of repression fail, the result may be the formation of neurotic *symptoms.*

Mental contents which are unconscious are irrationally rather than logically organized around wishes or drives, and strive for immediate discharge regardless of reality conditions. Thus we say that events in the dynamic unconscious are regulated by the *primary process* and the *pleasure principle.*

The dynamic unconscious is roughly coterminous with the structural system *'id'* but also includes important functions of the *ego* and *superego.*

C. **The 'System' Unconscious:** A region of the mental apparatus, topographically considered, in which memory traces are organized by primitive modes of associations (i.e. *primary process*). See *consciousness, preconscious, topography.*

WORKING THROUGH: A term originally used by Freud to describe the continuing application of analytic work to overcome *resistances* persisting after the initial *interpretation* of repressed instinctual *impulses.* He explained this 'id resistance' as a likely occurrence in view of the fact that an instinctual process which has been going along a particular path for decades is suddenly expected to take a new path that has just been made open for it. It is the goal of working through to make insight effective, i.e., to bring about significant and lasting changes in the patient by altering the modes and aims of the *instinctual drives.* This leads eventually to the inclusion of warded-off components in the total personality. Now considered a most important part of the analytic process, working through consists essentially of a repetition, extension, and deepening of the analysis of the resistances, which need to bc overcome repetitively and progressively. Both the patient and the analyst contribute to this task; it may be merely a repetition and elaboration of the usual analytic work or require special interventions in some cases. A special need for working through may exist when there has been a combination of traumatic experiences in early childhood and some event in latency which tends to organize and perpetuate the psychic reaction to the earlier trauma. Despite initial improvement, unless these traumatic events are thoroughly worked through, therapeutic changes will not be maintained and the patient will relapse.

AN INTRODUCTORY BIBLIOGRAPHY ON PSYCHOANALYSIS

ARLOW, J. *The Legacy of Freud.* New York: International Universities Press, 1956.

BRENNER, C. *An Elementary Textbook of Psychoanalysis.* New York: International Universities Press, 1955. A102 Anchor.

FRAIBERG, S. *The Magic Years. Understanding and Handling the Problems of Early Childhood.* New York: Scribner, 1959.

FREUD, A. *Psychoanalysis for Teachers and Parents.* New York: Emerson Books, Inc., 1935. BP109 Beacon Press.

FREUD, A. *Normality and Pathology in Childhood.* New York: International Universities Press, 1965.

FREUD, S. (1901) *The Psychopathology of Everyday Life.* MD67 NAL Mentor.

FREUD, S. (1915-1917) *General Introduction to Psychoanalysis.* Washington Square Press.

FREUD, S. (1933) *New Introductory Lectures on Psychoanalysis.* Norton, 1961.

HARTMANN, H., KRIS E., LOEWENSTEIN, R. M. Some Psychoanalytic Comments on 'Culture and Personality.' In: *Psychoanalysis and Culture,* ed. G. B. Wilbur and W. Muensterberger. New York: International Universities Press, 1951.

JONES, E. *The Life and Work of Sigmund Freud,* 3 Vols. New York: Basic Books, 1953. Abridged edition, ed. by L. Trilling and S. Marcus. A 340 Anchor.

KOHUT, H. and SEITZ, D. Psychoanalytic Theory of Personality. In: *Concepts of Personality,* ed. by J. M. Wepman and R. W. Heine. Chicago Aldine Press, 1963.

LEWIN, B. and ROSS, H. *Psychoanalytic Education in the United States.* New York: Norton, 1960.

LOEWENSTEIN, R. *Christians and Jews: A Psychoanalytic Study.* New York: International Universities Press, 1952.

PUMPIAN-MINDLIN, E. Ed. *Psychoanalysis and Science:* the Hickson Lectures on the Scientific Status of Psychoanalysis. New York: Basic Books, 1956.

REXFORD, E. Ed. *A Developmental Approach to Problems of Acting Out.* Monograph No. 1 of the *Journal of the American Academy of Child Psychiatry.* New York: International Universities Press, 1966.

WAELDER, R. *Basic Theory of Psychoanalysis.* New York: International Universities Press, 1960. SB80 Schocken Books.

INDEX OF TERMS NOT SEPARATELY DEFINED

INDEX OF TERMS NOT SEPARATELY DEFINED

INDEX OF TERMS NOT SEPARATELY DEFINED

INDEX OF TERMS NOT SEPARATELY DEFINED